TEN STUPID THINGS
WOMEN DO TO
MESS UP THEIR LIVES

Also by Dr. Laura C. Schlessinger in Large Print:

Ten Stupid Things Men Do to Mess Up
  Their Lives

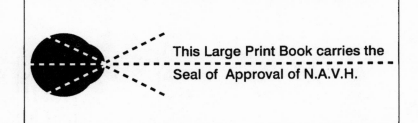

TEN STUPID THINGS WOMEN DO TO MESS UP THEIR LIVES

Dr. Laura C. Schlessinger

G.K. Hall & Co. • Thorndike, Maine

Published in 1998 by arrangement with Random House, Inc.

G.K. Hall Large Print Paperback Series.

The text of this Large Print edition is unabridged.
Other aspects of the book may vary from the original edition.

Set in 16 pt. Plantin by Minnie B. Raven.

Printed in the United States on permanent paper.

Library of Congress Cataloging in Publication Data

Schlessinger, Laura.
    Ten stupid things women do to mess up their lives / Laura
Schlessinger.
       p. cm.
    Large print ed.
    Originally published : 1st HarperPerennial ed. New York :
HarperPerennial, 1995.
    ISBN 0-7838-0396-6 (lg. print : sc : alk. paper)
    1. Man–woman relationships.   2. Women — Psychology.
I. Title.
HQ801.S4365   1998
155.3′33—dc21   98-40602

To my husband, Lew Bishop,
and my son, Deryk,
who never stopped telling me
I was the "little engine that could."

With all my love.

PREFACE

It ever has been since time began,
  And ever will be, till time lose breath,
That love is a mood — no more — to man,
  And love to a woman is life or death.

Ella Wheeler Wilcox
1850–1919

My hope is that this book will help both men and women put love and work in more harmonious balance; hence, learn to live together with more joy and meaning.

ACKNOWLEDGMENTS

I don't have any "little people" to thank. I have been fortunate to have had support, pushes, pulls, and nudges by many people of immense talent, heart, and friendship. I have regrets that I may not have always demonstrated the appreciation they deserved. I hope in these words, and in my life's actions, I show them all the respect, love, and gratitude they earned.

Dr. Bernard Abbott, once chairman of the Department of Biological Sciences at USC, gave me my first big break. After sending me a pleasant "Sorry, we don't have any permanent, full-time positions available," he responded with great humor to my follow-up call, "Okay, but might you have some not-so permanent, part-time position?" That preceeded five wonderful years as an assistant professor teaching biology, physiology, and human sexuality.

It was the last course that helped me discover my interest in psychotherapy.

Thanks, then, to Dr. Carlfred Broderick, director of the USC Human Relations Center. What makes him remarkable and memorable to me is that he didn't "impose" ideas; he excavated my mind and heart to have me see and accept and nurture what might be special in me. He was the beginning of my self-confidence.

Marcia Lasswell, current president of the American Association of Marriage and Family Therapists, was my mentor, teacher, supervisor, and role model. She is the most incredible combination of womanly charm, beauty, decisive wit, and intellect. Her energy is boundless, and her commitment and accomplishments in the field of marriage and family are legendary.

Dr. Jim Hedstrom, chairman of the graduate program in psychology at Pepperdine, gave me the opportunity to teach, therefore to truly learn my craft. He is a man of heart and integrity and gentle understanding.

Running parallel with my academic and professional growth was my introduction to its practical application: radio and, inevitably, this book. This interface belongs to Bill Ballance, the pioneer and "father" of personal-style talk radio. He literally "discovered me on the phone" and put me on his daily L.A. radio program once a week. No matter how many times I wanted to quit out of fear and self-doubt, he kept me going.

Time-out came when I decided to withdraw from the fray to produce and nurture the next miracle in my life, my son, Deryk. When Deryk was three I got back on the microphone on KWNK, walking distance from my house, thanks to the warmest, mushiest guy, sometimes disguised as a curmudgeon, Manny Cabranes.

From that jump start back into my professional life, I landed on KFI AM 640 thanks to George Oliva, then program director. I started on Sundays, then weekends, then six nights a week till 1:00 A.M., until the current program director, David G. Hall, switched me to middays . . . just to prove I wasn't a vampire and could be out in sunlight! I owe them both. David is my boss and friend — only he would know how to balance those so well.

Larry Metzler is my radio board operator and dear friend. He helped me keep my book and thoughts organized by producing "dubs" of significant calls for me to review. While I'm doing my show, his input during commercial breaks and news keeps up my spirits and, therefore, improves my performance. "Couldn't have done this without ye, Larry!" He's also been there when I've had a hurt in my heart.

The rest of my on-air team includes Susanne Whatley, news anchor, and Mark Denis, traffic reports. We've become a great team and great friends.

My therapy colleagues for closing in on two decades, Dr. Rhoda Marcovitch and Dr. Judith Friedman, have been there as creative critics and, more important, friends. I finally feel I have friends for life. There are so many times I could not have gotten through without them.

My husband, Lew Bishop, requires special attention here. Sometimes I think he's just crazy, because I can't fathom the magnitude of his uninterrupted love, loyalty, faith, friendship, and unrelenting efforts in behalf of my career. And Deryk thinks he's just the "best daddy" going.

Suzanne Wickham from Random House just called me one day and said, "You have a book in you. Write it!" I'd been scared to write a book — something about the exposure to criticism and judgment, I think. However, her positiveness and enthusiasm got me through the worst of it. Now I can't wait to start on the next!

Carolyn Fireside, my editor, is a special human being as well as an incredible professional. Before she got started with her red pencil, she listened to hours of tapes and read volumes of my writings to get to know me, my style, my voice, my message. She edited this book honoring all of those, making all the suggestions and improvements that made this a finished product about which I have great pride. Thank you, Carolyn.

Writing this acknowledgment section has been like counting my blessings. I am blessed. I am grateful.

— L. C. Schlessinger, 1993

CONTENTS

This book is going to be difficult for you to read — and maybe even hurtful to you — and you may get angry.

There are ten million exceptions to everything I say. Nonetheless, **EVERYTHING I SAY IS TRUE!**

INTRODUCTION

This is not a self-help book, but it will help women help themselves. Sound like double-talk? Kindly read on!

Here's another apparent contradiction. The inspiration for *Ten Stupid Things Women Do to Mess Up Their Lives* comes from two male sources: the first engineer on my KFI AM 640 Los Angeles call-in radio program, and my father.

First, the engineer. After working with me for more than six months, three hours a night, five days a week, Dan Mandis was hearing approximately twenty-five women per show agonize over "some dumb guy." "You know, Laura," he told me in an unguarded moment. "If you listen to your show long enough, you begin to think women are stupid!"

In my psychotherapeutic, compassionate, non-judgmental opinion, that comment amounted to heresy. Yet after a while, I began to wonder if there was some truth to it. Yes, we are motivated by unrealistic drives and primal needs related to yearnings for a paradise-never-visited in childhood. And yes, practicalities sometimes make our choices and directions seem almost too complex to fathom, much less handle. That's part and parcel of the human condition. But I had to admit that women knowingly do stupid things — like using complaining, whining, anger, depression, anxiety, food, and chemicals to avoid taking active steps to improve their lot. They "cop out." They get "chicken." *They act stupid.*

An example: One of my callers, who was "having trouble" losing weight, claimed that she had looked in every available self-help book for a scenario she could really relate to. She called because she was frustrated she hadn't found it yet.

Oh, great! In other words, until she finds herself in a book (which I bet will never happen), she has a perfect excuse for doing nothing — and that "nothing" includes confronting the fact that she is basically lazy. Her goal in life may be to look like a model, which could be foolish and unrealistic in itself, but she's totally unwilling to put in any effort whatsoever to achieve it.

Granted, there are no psychiatric diagnostic categories for laziness, immaturity, cowardice, selfishness, and downright stupidity. Even if there were, it wouldn't matter because no one bothers to consider them anymore. Know why? In the Age of the Victim, nothing is anybody's fault! All the personality and behavioral traits I just listed have been swept clean away as women, aided and abetted by a torrent of apologetic self-help books, insist on rationalizing their self-destructive behavior by identifying themselves as "sick." Codependent, addicted, loved too much, scarred by a dysfunctional past, whatever — we've provided ourselves with a virtual boutique of new "identities" designed to enable us to marinate in our weaknesses.

Listen to Dr. Laura! For improvement to happen, these weaknesses need airing and exercising. Until you take them on, you are a victim. And you don't have to be a female rocket scientist to figure out who the perpetrator is! Dan the engineer — a man — could tell you in a second. It's you! That's what he meant when he said women seemed stupid. The ultimate stupidity is withholding from yourself the respect you deserve.

Bottom line: If you want a higher self-esteem, there's only one, admittedly old-fashioned, way to get it: Earn it!

On to the second motivation for this book: my father, who once remarked at dinner that men couldn't get away with anything rotten, political or personal, unless women let them. He listed every conceivable transgression — petty robbery, abuse, war, governmental corruption, you name it. According to his argument, the ultimate power of women over men was their sexual acceptance and/or approval.

My father loved to bait me, especially at the dinner table, so I must have made his day when I immediately became outraged at the very notion that men would shunt off responsibility for their actions. As with Dan's comment, though, I continued to ponder the possibility that there might be some truth to my father's theory. A woman, I reasoned, is not responsible for a man's choices. She is, however, responsible for her own — which too often entail tolerating some obnoxious male behaviors in order to avoid, for example, loneliness, self-assertiveness, and self-sufficiency.

If, from the first meeting with an ill-mannered lout, a woman expressed her disdain clearly and confidently, the guy would either shape up or expect to get shipped out. If, instead, she focuses on her dependency and desperate need for male acceptance while forgetting about his dependency and craving for approval and then continues to be sexually receptive, she'll be giving him a strong signal that she condones his behavior. So I have to concede my father had a point. Unfortunately, now that he's passed on, this intellectual arm-wrestle is history.

By the way, I'm aware that women psychologists are generally mistrusted by men as male-bashers. If any of you guys are sneaking a peek at this book, you can relax. If anything, I'm woman-bashing! And get ready, women, because I'm taking off the gloves and telling you the naked truth. You can take it. You need to hear it.

Here goes. Men are not keeping you miserable. You are! If you are unhappy with your man, straighten yourself out and pick better! Put all this low self-esteem stuff in perspective. Life is hard. Only those willing to sustain themselves through self-doubt and difficult periods of pain, loss, even dread, will achieve enhanced self-respect. It's that simple.

If you don't want to put in the effort, accept that you've made a decision not to grow. If changing is simply too much trouble, just forget it — and at least give yourself some peace. If you're bent on excusing your inner weakness and passivity by spending decades "recovering," go right ahead. It's your life. If you're more interested in helping yourself than in so-called self-help, which means eternally searching for a miracle cure via the latest guru's new cop-out title-of-the-month, this is the book for you!

Women, rebel! Don't fall for yet another slick explanation of the pathetic yet understandable motivation for your weak-kneed behavior. My book was written to encourage you to show yourself what you're made of. And when you do, I guarantee you, you'll be impressed!

Ten Stupid Things Women Do to Mess Up Their Lives is not about steps, syndromes, or programs. It's not about "recovery." It's not a "miracle cure" for your problems that promises gain without pain.

This book is intended to open your eyes, startle you into awareness, and smarten you up.

But it will not do the trick for all women.

Some of you will resent it, even reject it, because "looking in the mirror" does not always reflect a "pretty picture" and because confronting your own stupidity can really hurt. You may even know I'm right but still not be consciously ready to take an objective look at yourself.

So feel free to hurl the fruit of my labors across the room or call it nasty names or just ignore it. Just, please, for your own good, keep it around!

Because someday, when things get bad enough and the pain and feelings of helplessness get too acute to bear, you'll go to it. And it will be there for you as you make your most important decision ever: to fight your way out of misery and go take on your life!

1. Stupid Attachment

IS A WOMAN JUST A WO- WO- WO- ON A MAN?

I remember precisely when I knew I had to write this book. It was a few years ago when my husband, Lew, and I were leaving a screening of Robin Williams's *Dead Poets Society*. The movie, you may recall, concerns the students and faculty of an exclusive boys' school and is set in the fifties. So? What's the big deal? Not exactly the subject to inspire strong emotions in a nineties woman, yet I found myself deeply upset — and equally puzzled because my feelings did seem so way out of proportion to the specific dramatic events of the film.

As I struggled to understand my "overreaction," I found myself focusing on my anger at the mother of the main student in the film, a sensitive sort, whose father refuses to allow him to follow his dream of a career in the theater! The boy is to be a doctor, the father froths, and that's that!

While the father declaims, the mother just sits in a corner suffering in silence. She watches the complete demoralization of her son, yet does nothing. Before she dutifully follows her husband to his bed, she gently hugs the boy, pats him solemnly on the back, and then walks away sadly.

The young man uses his father's gun to kill himself.

I went absolutely crazy with pain.

That a mother could stand by and allow the selfish insensitivity of her husband to destroy her own child absolutely horrified me.

By the time my husband and I reached the parking lot, I had worked myself up into a rage at the character's weakness, her cowardice, her subservience. In fact, I held her more responsible for the boy's death than the father!

The father was all caught up in his competitive macho behavior of using his son as his ego extension. After all, could being a doctor be considered such a bad thing to wish on someone?

But the mother knew her son's heart. She knew he had poetry in his heart, which did not need a stethoscope over it.

She just would not stand up to her controlling husband.

A middle-aged woman who was parked next to us heard me railing and anguishing over the mother's spineless culpability and took it upon herself to calm me down. "Well," she said firmly, "that's just how women were in those . . . my . . . days!" Her tone actually seemed quite sympathetic toward the servile woman of forty years ago; and that made me even angrier and sadder.

BOYS YEARN FOR COURAGE AND NO "CHAPTER 11" . . . WHILE GIRLS YEARN FOR CURLS AND NO CELLULITE

As my husband and I drove home, my mood became even more melancholy as I continued to ruminate. I surprised even myself with this next observation: "You know, Lew, *Dead Poets Society* could not have been written about a girls school — whether it was set in the fifties or now! It is a movie about ideals and aspirations, about personal discovery by courageous actions, not just by attending 'Adult Children of Some Kind of Imperfect Parent' organization.

"Let me ask you something. If the movie was set in a girls prep school, would anybody 'buy' it? Would it make sense? Would it make the point the author was trying to make?

My husband thought for a moment, then told me, "No, I guess not."

ARE YOU JUST A WO- WO- WO- ON A MAN?

His agreement about the obviousness of this sad truth made me feel tearful, profoundly sad, frustrated, angry, and ashamed both at women and for women — women as personified by my comforter in the parking lot. Women possibly like your mother or aunt, your teacher or female friends, maybe even like yourself, who use an entire arsenal of excuses to avoid facing the fact that they define themselves and their role in the world exclusively through men — and it almost "don't" matter what "kinda" man! (More about that later . . . much, much, much more.)

DON'T DISCOUNT THE POSITIVE ASPECTS OF MALE BEHAVIOR

In the nearly fifteen years I have worked with men and women in private practice and on radio, I am constantly amazed by how myopic women are about life and themselves, and how much they complain about men! I wonder if the absence of complaining about men would eliminate the talk show industry. Most of what you hear on these talk shows is whining about how men are unwilling to commit to women after minutes or millennia of dating.

Women seem to like more to whine about problems than to solve them. Men, more typically, want to solve problems rather than talk on and on about them. Men are being maligned because they are not behaving like women: Talk, talk, talk, whine, whimper, analyze, reanalyze, etc. Ugh.

To use a familiar saying, "Why can't a

woman be more like a man" is sometimes not such a bad idea. Women are so driven by the desire to exist through men that they miss the positive examples male behavior can offer them as a model.

Contrary to much of the feminist cant, there are many things we can learn from men's perspective about life and personal identity. To refuse to learn anything that could prove beneficial to yourself is a working definition of stupid. I sincerely believe that if women studied male lessons in concepts of assertion, courage, destiny, purpose, honor, dreams, endeavor, perseverance, goal orientation, etc., they would have a more fulfilling life, pick better men with whom to be intimate, and have better relationships with them.

"I AM BARBIE, SEE MY HAIR GROW!"

Of course, there are already special, spectacular women out there who were born and/or imbued with a strong sense of personal destiny — you may even be one of them. Generally, aspirations and lofty intentions don't dovetail with women's concept of femininity, because the determination to make your life extraordinary is not a typical part of female thinking. To be completely honest, there is no realization of dreams and purpose for either women or men without difficulty, opposition, disappointment, and failure. When the French say, *"La vie est dure,"* life is hard, it pertains to everyone who's ever lived, not just womankind. In order to grow, you've got to face the fact that painless change happens only in fairy tales.

So stop blaming men or society or anything else for your personal disappointments. Decide to become more meaningful to yourself and to others. Then you can go take on the day every day of your life.

THE "HIGH" PRICE OF "LOW" FEMALE SELF-ESTEEM

The price for not making a move toward personal specialness has always been and continues to be too great. Since women do not typically define self-esteem and purpose in terms of personal accomplishment, the ways they have gone about getting some sense of identity, value, and meaning in their lives have been primarily through relationships. That has been disappointing and destructive. In the 1830s Lord Byron wrote, "For men, love is a thing apart, for women it is their whole existence."

Unfortunately, it is still all too true today.

"WE HAVEN'T COME A LONG ENOUGH WAY, BABY!"

Whitney Houston was quoted in the *Los Angeles Times* (11/22/92 — that's 1992, not 1892) as having said, "Women are supposed to have husbands. We are validated by that, and we validate ourselves that way."

Even today, on the eve of the twenty-first century, there are young women for whom the very possibility that there is life separate from attachment to some guy comes as a revelation. Read these amazing a *Los Angeles Times* article (11/2/93) called "New Rules for Teen Love": ". . . she never had thought it possible for a girl to spend a Saturday night without a date — and still be happy: 'I grew up thinking that if you're not with [some guy], you're nothing. Then, last Saturday I went with Michelle to the movies. I couldn't believe it was fun to go out with girls.' "

A twinkle of hope? Well, perhaps, but . . .

A thirty-one-year-old woman who has had affairs with athletes in two sports said this to *Time* magazine (11/25/91): "For women, many of whom don't have meaningful work, the only way to identify themselves is to say whom they have slept with. A woman who sleeps around is called a whore. But a woman who has slept with Magic Johnson is a woman who has slept with Magic Johnson. It's almost as if it gives her legitimacy."

So here it is — nothing new — identity through attachment to a man perceived as super-special. And God help you if that perception changes, because once the star falls from grace, so does the woman's sense of worth. She simply ceases to exist. It's no wonder that so many women get furious with their men for having even reasonable human frailties and don't "stand by their man" during the harder times.

MATHEMATICS 1: MARRIAGE DOES NOT EQUAL SELF-WORTH

"And now, from Santa Clarita, Susan, you're on KFI," the conversation began. And Susan, twenty-nine, came on the line by telling me she'd been married for five and a half months but still felt an overwhelming sense of insignificance. Her husband, the marital state itself — well, things just hadn't turned out the way she'd imagined.

"Nothing in my life," she said mournfully, "affirms my worth to myself."

Think of it like this: If you bring your own goals and dreams and self-awareness to a marriage, the other person can be a tremendous source of comfort and support when your career or one of your friendships is going through a rough patch. That's true for anything that causes your ego to suffer a blow — and you can and should do the same for your partner.

If you bring to the relationship nothing but your neediness, the balance is all off. You become your husband's baby, his perpetual "damsel in distress." Though a damsel may be macho-assuaging for a while, it is not long before she becomes a constant emotional drain and a total "taker."

In such a lopsided situation, you're bound to feel lonely, because feelings of self-worth do not come from the mere existence or presence of someone in your life. Counting on that, in fact, just makes the pain of your sense of personal nothingness even worse.

WANT SELF-ESTEEM? GET IT THE OLD-FASHIONED WAY . . . EARN IT!

On this very important subject of self-esteem, social psychologist Carol Tavris makes a valid point when she writes that self-esteem is now a mere shadow of its former self. "Once," she claims, "it referred to a fundamental sense of self-worth; today that meaning has narrowed into merely feeling good about oneself. Self-esteem used to rest on the daily acts of effort, care and accomplishment that are the bedrock of character; now it rests on air, on being instead of doing."

So when women stuck in Susan's depressed, low-self-esteem quagmire ask: "How can I increase my self-esteem? Can you recommend a book? A seminar? A workshop? A group?" here's my answer: Self-esteem is earned! When you dare to dream, dare to follow that dream, dare to suffer through the pain, sacrifice, self-doubts, and friction from the world — when you show such courage and tenacity — you will genuinely impress yourself. And most important, you will treat yourself accordingly and not settle for less from others — at least, not for long.

Self-esteem is always forged from your efforts. I still cannot believe the self-defeating moves women make to avoid those efforts.

A LOUSY RELATIONSHIP IS NEVER BETTER THAN NO RELATIONSHIP AT ALL

Vanessa, a twenty-seven-year-old caller, was furious that her physically and verbally abusive boyfriend had broken off with her to go back to his ex-girlfriend, whom he had also abused.

What astonished me was that Vanessa wasn't calling in anger about his abuse. She called because she was angry that he decided to leave!

I said to her, with some irony, "If you took all that crap, at least he should be giving it only to you!" She came back with "I know," and giggled!

Vanessa continued, "I gave so much away. And my self-acceptance was based on his acceptance of me. I just don't understand why he's done what he's done."

Here she had taken all this abuse, hoping this would ensure his undying love and attachment, and it didn't work. What a blow!

When I suggested that Vanessa tell me about

her goals, to name only one, she couldn't. When I talked to her about hard work and sacrifice as a means of building something special, she dismissed the whole idea by claiming she guessed she was just lazy.

I asked her if all this *sturm und drang* of the relationship with this crazy guy was "exciting." She giggled again, and admitted that it was. "The fighting, the making up, the wondering, the pain. It is pretty exciting in a way. Certainly takes up my life."

This is what you call a life?

DON'T EXPECT A MAN TO SHARE YOUR "ALL-FOR-LOVE" ATTITUDE

I sincerely hope I helped Vanessa see a little light by chipping away at her denial. I sincerely hope I helped you see a little more clearly, too. It just seems such a tragic waste to see young women suffering needlessly by having no independent goals, to observe them acting so stupidly. I can't tell you how many twenty-something women I've talked to over the years who are furious with the young men in their lives who don't want to get married just yet because they're working practically full-time getting their education and/or building their careers. If you're one of these women, take his hint — or follow his example! Because, as I've said, men do have traits we'd be smart to adapt.

31

THE GOOD LIFE REQUIRES GUTS

Let me describe a fantastic cartoon — by a male, Jules Feiffer. A man meets a guru in the road. The man asks the guru, "Which way is success?" The berobed, bearded sage speaks not but points to a place off in the distance. The man, thrilled by the prospect of quick and easy success, rushes off in the appropriate direction. Suddenly, there comes a loud "SPLAT." Eventually, the man limps back, tattered and stunned, assuming he must have misinterpreted the message. He repeats his question to the guru, who again points silently in the same direction. The man obediently walks off once more. This time the splat is deafening, and when the man crawls back, he is bloody, broken, tattered, and irate. "I asked you which way is success," he screams at the guru. "I followed the direction you indicated. And all I got was splatted! No more of this pointing! Talk!" Only then does the guru speak, and what he says is this: "Success *is* that way. Just a little *past* splat."

Accomplishment, leading to self-esteem, is not just about doing something. . . . It is about the courage to persist through pain and failure and self-doubt; to go past splat.

I've lost count of all the callers who give sad testimony to the extraordinary and wholly inappropriate "romantic" situations in which women find themselves because they have never found the courage to go past splat, to focus on self-effort as the avenue to self-esteem and positive identity.

I can just feel that ultra-feminists reading this want to knock me upside my head right about now with some complaint that women just haven't been able to do important things because men haven't let them. While I'm not going to deny the realities of the male power structure, I do want to reprimand you sternly about passing the buck. I recently spoke to a group of educated, accomplished women who belong to a group called American Association of University Women. The approach of the meeting had to do with what stood in the way of women accomplishing more.

The irony was deafening. Here I am, surrounded by hundreds of successful women of all ages and races who managed to do it. Why aren't we studying them?

Obviously, it can be done. If, if, if, you're not lazy or cowardly.

THERE OUGHT TO BE A LAW AGAINST ROMANTIC ENTRAPMENT

Tragically, when a woman doesn't dare to dream or endeavor to a purpose, a sense of meaning generally comes from excessive emphasis on a relationship with a man and/or producing babies — sometimes even using the latter to ensure the former. Perhaps the most shocking (and unhappy) proponent of this approach was Jennifer, age twenty-two, from Glendale.

Jennifer tearfully reported that she'd "been with" her fiancé for two years, although they weren't living together. Now she was pregnant, but when she told the daddy, he was furious and wanted her to have an abortion. She was distraught that the relationship had turned upside down, that her man was terribly disturbed about the baby and felt betrayed . . .

Basically, though, her call was about her being angry with him!

DR. LAURA: Were you guys using contraception?

JENNIFER: Well, I was taking the Pill, but I went off it when I decided to —

DR. LAURA: — decided to get pregnant intentionally?

JENNIFER: Um . . . yes. . . . He wanted to go to school and get a better job before we got married and I didn't want to wait four or five years.

DR. LAURA: I can't believe this, Jennifer. Do you realize you did a terrible thing?

JENNIFER: Well, yeah . . . but . . .

DR. LAURA: Forget the "but"! When you unilaterally decide to trick someone — even when you think it's out of love — they're well within their right not to trust you and not to feel the same way about you.

JENNIFER: But how can I be happy with myself, about the baby?

DR. LAURA: That's a tough one. This pregnancy was never about becoming a mother or being a family. It was about coercing and manipulating somebody into changing his life before he was committed to the change. And the reason you did it is because you don't have a life outside of what you thought being married would give you. I know I'm telling you things you don't want to hear. But I doubt I'm telling you things you don't already know.

If you realize you're not ready to be a mom and he's unwilling to be a dad, you might want to think of adoption as an option, so that this child will be raised by a loving couple who truly want it, are ready for it, and can take care of it.

JENNIFER: I just don't know what I need to do to make things better . . .

DR. LAURA: Now, he may not want to marry you, but he is the father of a child, whether it was his plan or not. You forced him to be a dad when he didn't feel ready. I don't know how all of this is going to turn out between you. But you need to pick yourself up in a spurt of maturity and take full responsibility for what you've done and realize how frightened you are in anticipating a grown-up life that you would go to this end.

That is not what being a wife is about, or

mother, or grown-up. You're pregnant right now, so you have big decisions to make, and being angry with him for not "falling into place" is not the kind of thinking you need to do.

His angry reaction is reasonable and you need to tell him so.

JENNIFER: I need to tell him I betrayed, tricked him?

DR. LAURA: You can't be truthful with him and yet you want to marry him? Listen, the hallmark of a marriage, of any intimate relationship, is truth, especially about your weaknesses and vulnerabilities. You know what I think? I think this guy would be crazy to marry you right now. If you want his attitude to change, first tell him you're terribly sorry. Then commit to being honest — with him and with yourself. Admit to the truth of your fears, and take them where they belong, to a counselor. You've got to stop acting out and deal directly with your dread of not having an identity. These fears are things we can talk through, survive, and grow from. And remember, Jennifer, you have no real future with your fiancé at all — unless you start with the truth!

YOU CAN'T SHARE WHAT YOU DON'T HAVE, AND THAT GOES DOUBLY FOR RESPONSIBILITY

When she rang off, Jennifer sounded a lot more centered and resolved than she had at the beginning of our encounter. But you may be thinking I was too hard on her, that her anger with her boyfriend wasn't entirely unjustified; after all, he was engaging in a sexual relationship with her, and he knew that sexuality brings risk along with the pleasure. The birth-control pill does have a 2 percent failure rate, which means that of one hundred women using the birth-control pill for one year, two will become pregnant. This is the actual *vs.* theoretical failure rate, which is smaller because it doesn't include human error.

In fact, if the fiancé had called, angrily condemning his girlfriend for having gotten pregnant while on the Pill and interrupting his personal life's plans (and I have gotten many such calls from men), I would have told him that regardless of whether his girlfriend got pregnant because the Pill failed or she failed to take the Pill, he is responsible for his own sperm! His plans now need to include fatherhood. When adults are sexually active, they assume responsibility for the risks and consequences.

I intentionally didn't mention this shared responsibility to Jennifer because I wanted to emphasize what her responsibilities were. I wanted to stress to her, and to listeners identifying with her personal fears of life and autonomy, that any and all decisions and actions intended to manipulate men into enforced caretaking are unconscionable, cowardly, selfish, and destructive. End of story.

You'll read more about this terrible ploy in a later chapter, but it's still only one of the stupid ways in which women mess up their lives.

OBSESSIONS AND MARTYRDOM (UNPAID SOCIAL WORK) ARE WOEFULLY INEFFECTIVE HEDGES AGAINST FEMALE AUTONOMY

Are you obsessed with your weight, your thighs, your breasts, the thinness of your hair? If they were only different, you'd be loved?

Sylvia did have a real physical problem: male-pattern baldness in women. She was quite self-conscious about this rare medical problem and was working with a physician to get it under control.

Understandably, she felt uncomfortable about her looks, but the degree of her concern was obsessive: the reading, buying, trying, worrying, remedies, etc.

I asked her when she seemed to focus in on her hair problem the most.

Sylvia admitted, "I've been trying to go to school for the last five years and I've been having problems with that. I work and go to school and it's hard. And it's a difficult course — court reporting. And it's hard to concentrate sometimes; it just doesn't come easy to me."

I explained that when things are tough, stressful, scary, it's sometimes a lot easier to find other things to worry about rather than do your work. There is no surprise there. Every college student knows that feeling and the games of procrastination and distraction.

"When you're stressed," I told her, "you obsess." I also suggested that she fight through the discomfort of having to work hard, of feeling different. I offered that she needed to be more positive in her attitude and have more fun in her life.

Obsessing about imperfections makes for low self-evaluation, obviously. And just like water seeks its own level, equal self-evaluations match up in men and women, too. It just doesn't seem to be obvious.

There are legions of women who stay with men who are drug or alcohol abusers, and/or who are immature and irresponsible, and/or who betray trust emotionally, sexually, and financially, and/or who aren't loyal or supportive — who basically are not one of the good guys who are out there.

Generally, you discover these realities early on in the relationship — and that realization is the seductive hook that reels you in instead of signaling you to run for cover.

By continuing the relationship, you — out of cowardice and self-denial — short-circuit your progress toward "purpose" by martyring yourself on the altar of someone else's pain or need. Therein lies the appeal — the probability that the guy will "stay with you" because of his dependency on your caretaking. Between his dependency and your "mission," you have an identity and a sense of security, however skewed, which eventually leads you to be non-sexually screwed.

WHEN YOU DEVOTE YOUR LIFE TO "FINDING YOURSELF," YOU PROBABLY WON'T

Yet another style of struggling with purpose and identity is to bury your head in the sand, run away, and just keep putting off commitment to some purpose in any form! That was the case with Sibella, a thirty-year-old who called from Santa Monica.

Sibella was trying to decide whether to move to Germany, where she would be living with a boyfriend and taking a philosophical/spiritual seminar, or to stay in California and start a career. The only catch was that she hadn't a clue about what kind of career to start. She admitted to me that she felt she hadn't really ever achieved anything, despite the fact that all her life she'd been told she had tremendous potential . . .

DR. LAURA: Pretty scary, huh? To finally have to test that potential?

SIBELLA: Yeah, and it's funny . . . I am not — at least I think I'm not — afraid of failure.

DR. LAURA: Oh man, then you are the only person on the face of the earth who isn't. That's a fib, Sibella, but nice try. And I'll tell you, one of the things women types do when they get in this kind of predicament is to go live with a boyfriend while he does "his thing," which they ultimately come to resent as a competitor for attention. You're just postponing, postponing, postponing.

SIBELLA: Yes. And it's because . . . well . . . I've done a lot of soul-searching, but I feel I still don't know the real purpose of life.

DR. LAURA: You make purpose each day. I see the purpose of life when I look into my boy's sweet face. I feel the purpose of my life when I get on the phones here at KFI and have a conversation with someone, and feel it might have helped either the caller or some listener.

Perhaps the purpose of life is forged moment by moment. If you're going to wait till you find something "bigger than that" before you do anything, then you're doing a sixties kind of "I can't do anything till I find myself." And, my love, the nothingness you are giving, doing, and creating is yourself.

SIBELLA: Yes, exactly!

DR. LAURA: That is an avoidance of life. Life

41

is not a coordinated complete picture of any kind for anyone. It is creating something for every day as best you can.

SIBELLA: And yet most people go through life with a goal in mind or something specific in their heart.

DR. LAURA: I think most people go through life trying to figure out how to survive each day. A goal? Build a Taj Mahal. A goal? Give someone else hope. A goal? Learn something new, exciting, and then wonder about a new and special use for it.

SIBELLA: And so basically you just think it's a matter of getting over the fear? I'm just procrastinating?

DR. LAURA: That's a pretty big "just!" Sibella, you've got to commit to something. I'm not telling you it has to be your life's dream or that it'll get you a Nobel Prize. But it will earn you more ownership of yourself. Commit to something — that is the essence of soul-searching. You're not soul-searching now, you're ruminating over fears of negative judgment and failure, disguised as search for "the ultimate wisdom."

Stop it. Do something.

SIBELLA: And give up the possibility of everything else I might have found or done?

DR. LAURA: Honey, anything you do leaves out everything else at that one moment. But it's also called having a moment of some depth in your life, where you do have some meaning. While I am here with you I am not riding my bicycle — I had to give up the possibility of that journey to have a new one with you — touching another human being. I'll settle for that.

SIBELLA: Yes, me too, thank you.

I hope I helped Sibella understand that if identity is going to come only from doing that right special something, then the something becomes the everything. When identity comes from the doing, the something becomes secondary. Baking bread is as glorious as planting flowers, as doing a cardiac bypass, as teaching a child to read.

The moral of this story is to not get stuck in looking for the right thing to do, the outstanding thing that will make you special. It is the process of doing, of committing yourself to something that makes the difference in your enjoyment of life and your satisfaction with self.

The same thinking applies to the fear of settling for one man when the next one might be better. This is not the thinking of a person ready, willing, and able to be caring and committed. It's the thinking of a woman who hopes to find the miracle cure that will make her feel like a valid person, like a real woman. For many contemporary females, that hoped-for miracle continues too often to be an ill-timed, ill-selected, ill-planned marriage and motherhood.

THE FEMALE ESCAPE ROUTE: THE QUICKEST MEANS TO PAINT YOURSELF INTO A CORNER

Although I'm always aware of being a woman, the most womanly I have ever felt was when I was pregnant. Imagine, having life within your body; being able to make, sustain, nurture new life. How special and incredible!

Well, even beautiful, special things such as marriage and motherhood have their proper time and place and purpose. The problem is, many women simply want to hide there.

Just the other day, a patient, a young woman in her early thirties with three children, ages fourteen to three and a half, talked about her early family life, during which she and her sister were never expected, never encouraged, to think of their lives in terms of personal dreams. She used a phrase remarkable for its poignancy: "So, I took the female escape route and got married and made babies right out of high school."

At thirty-something, she is finally ready to "take on the world," constrained by a family she made too soon, and for the wrong reasons.

Some women get a bit luckier. They've got guys who don't want to be burdened with women who are in creative hiding.

Thirty-one-year-old Carol, who called from Hollywood, was a study in misery. She'd followed her boyfriend from Boston to L.A., where he was trying hard to make it in the music industry. After two months here, she had no job, no car, no friends, no family, no money. She hated it. Carol admitted freely she'd relocated with no commitment from the young man, who didn't even want to think about marriage and a family until he was established in his profession. She felt desperate by the failure of her pressuring to get him to give her access to the female escape route.

When I suggested to Carol that her boyfriend was right and that she ought to adopt his way of thinking, her tears, pain, and fear kept her from hearing me at first.

The breakthrough came when I asked her what her "dreams" were. First, she denied ever having any. Then she tearfully added, "Getting married and having children."

When I asked her what she was going to do with herself until then, she quietly said, "Nothing, I guess . . . nothing."

She said she had never had any dreams or goals. I doubt that was true, but I do believe she's just totally scared.

My advice to Carol was to move back to Boston and get an education. As it was, I told her that she was but a comma in the sentence of her boyfriend's life, while for her, he was the entire text! That brand of emotional imbalance is almost always a format for disaster.

WHEN YOU'RE READY TO CHANGE, YOU'LL HEED THE CALL

Some six months after this call, while taping a television appearance, I was approached by a young man who worked on the set. "You're Dr. Laura!" He beamed, shaking my hand enthusiastically. "My girlfriend from Boston called you about six months ago."

I remembered the girlfriend instantly! It was Carol.

"You know," he continued, "you told her what I'd been telling her. Only, she listened to you! I was so relieved."

He candidly admitted that although he really cared about Carol, she had become a burden. "I was trying to work toward my things and all she wanted me to do was to take care of her!"

"I know you'll be happy to hear," he continued, "that she did move back home to go to school. I want to thank you for both of us. Whew! And hurray!"

MARRIAGE AND MOTHERHOOD ARE FOR ADULTS ONLY

It's true that the good guys out there do want a total woman — not one who greets them at the front door wrapped in cellophane (on a daily basis, anyway), but a centered, self-aware human being who wants to, rather than needs

46

to, be with him as a companion, lover, friend, co-parent.

As a former male patient complained, men don't easily have the privilege of running from the fear of failure they have to do something (well, I guess they can become bums or "kept men"), while women can fall back into biology: make babies.

If I had tried to make my son my sole purpose in life, I'd probably have psychologically destroyed him with my overwhelming demand that he either fulfill my dreams or display such excellence that my craving for reflected identity would be satisfied. This same is true of my marriage, which is a joy and comfort, not an obsession or manifestation of neurotic neediness.

NOT SUPERWOMAN — JUST A SUPER WOMAN

It is your job as a woman, as a person, to become as fully realized as you can by having dreams, forging a purpose, building an identity, having courage, and making commitments to things outside yourself. In so doing, you take a more active role in the quality of your own life so that other people — friends, spouses, children — share in your growth rather than become responsible for it. You'll feel super. And you'll feel really womanly — as opposed to babyish or girlish — perhaps for the first time.

AND WHEN IT WORKS,
IT'S WONDERFUL

I am heartened to know that many of you have gotten the message. This follow-up letter from a caller is an example I'm particularly proud of:

Dr. Laura,
   One and a half years ago you helped me see what I knew already, and I broke off a bad relationship with a man. I also went to see a therapist, who helped me make better choices. I'm now dating a kind, giving, good man (for over a year) and we have a true relationship — complete with the gives and takes and compromises that are necessary for a strong friendship and a good base for a future. Thank you so much!
   I'm also building my career and making decisions for my future, not basing them on "what he is doing."

                                    Yours, Kitty.

It's letters like these that make me constantly realize not only how much I love what I do but that many, many women are ready to change. They just need a jump start to do it!

PERSONAL COURAGE GIVES YOU THE FREEDOM TO CHOOSE

Now, to sum up: When you choose to include ideals such as courage and personal achievement as part of your feminine identity, I'll stop hearing: "I know he lies (cheats, steals, whatever) — but I'm thirty-nine. What if I never find another guy?"

OR, "I know he's abusive to me and the kids. But I'm too afraid to be alone."

OR, "I know I should let go of him (or some compulsive behavior); it's just that I get too uncomfortable. I don't like that feeling. So I just give up."

OR many of the other traps women fall into because of their lack of recognition and exercise of their true grit. The chapters to come will deal with them.

So read and learn — and get ready to be challenged.

2. Stupid Courtship

"I FINALLY FOUND SOMEONE I COULD ATTACH TO" AND OTHER STUPID IDEAS ABOUT DATING

Problems that callers present on my radio program can sadden me, frustrate me, even upset me. But after some fifteen years of on- and off-air counseling experience, they rarely surprise me.

I was not initially surprised by this particular Saturday-night call . . . then . . .

HE'S A COMPLETE TURKEY, BUT WHY HASN'T HE CALLED?

Christine came across as a strong, positive, assertive young woman, who described her "first date from hell" as if we were two best girlfriends in a jocular, "you won't believe what happened next" mood.

She told me she'd gone to a party with a female friend but had begun talking with one particular fellow, who eventually suggested they go somewhere to talk. She agreed, left her friend to find her own way home (this behavior really

50

deserves its own chapter!), and accompanied her new companion to an all-night coffee shop.

Her description of the rest of the evening played like sound bites from a comedy special about the worst kind of blind or first date. The man smoked without asking her permission or even inquiring whether it bothered her. His smoking *did* bother her, and she told him so. Without consulting her or checking to see if she was hungry, he proceeded to order only coffee for them both. Not only did he talk about himself the entire time, he also performed a series of tacky magic tricks, which made Christine wish the earth would swallow her up, then discoursed on the profound significance of astrology as a personal life philosophy. He never asked her one interested question about herself.

As Christine talked about the evening, she and I continued to joke about her date's narcissism and boorishness. At this point, I assumed she had called to give evidence on how difficult it was to find a good man or, perhaps, to discuss how to unload such a rude and self-centered individual without seeming too rude or critical, since women tend to be overly concerned with appearing nice.

I was wrong. So wrong.

For when I asked her why she had called, her tone changed dramatically from that of a positive good ol' girl to a deflated, disappointed li'l girl.

"I wonder," she confessed, "if I shouldn't have mentioned anything about his cigarette smoking. He hasn't called me since that night. He did ask me for my number, but he hasn't called. I know where he works. Maybe I should call him?"

Was she kidding?

I don't think so!

DATING SHOULD BE ABOUT SELECTING, NOT BEING SELECTED

Like Christine, far too many women behave more like beggars than choosers in the dating game. For them, dating is a process of hoping-to-be-selected rather than an opportunity to select. For example:

Twenty-four-year-old Annette from L.A. called to complain about her tendency to choose "the wrong type" of man — which, at present, is a younger fellow of twenty-one. "Isn't that awful?" she asks, and when I inquire what's so awful about it, she replies that it is completely "inappropriate." "It's not just because of my age," she explains. "It's my social situation. I have a seven-year-old son, which makes me seem even older in comparison than I am chronologically." I concede that's a good point and then we get down to business.

GO WITH THE FLOW, AND YOU COULD GET CAUGHT IN THE UNDERTOW

What I tell Annette applies to many of you. We all tend to be motivated much too much by the tremendous relief that comes with realizing someone (read anyone) is interested in us — because we're lonely or feeling amorous and would like to act it out. So we go with the flow without, indeed, making any choice at all. Do you see the crucial difference there? Acquiescing to an availability is in no way making a choice.

I point out this fundamental distinction to Annette, stressing that what she needs to do is spend time thinking about what she really wants and needs at this particular time in her life. If, as it appears to me, she is inclined to be a family person and devote her energy to her son instead of to her social life, she has to be prepared to sustain herself through those low times we all go through when we feel alone.

SWEATING OUT THE ROUGH TIMES

How do we get through rough times? By believing in ourselves enough and occupying ourselves enough, developing ourselves enough, so that we can tolerate the discomfort between now and our next triumph. As I've said, there really is no gain without pain — emotionally as well as aerobically. Why not ride the loneliness through and come out a stronger person as the result of it? Why not fill our minds and our hearts and stop using a relationship with a man as a substitute for that core fulfillment?

DOWN WITH FAIRY TALES!

None of us, thank heaven, is Cinderella — who happens to be the greatest example ever of a woman waiting for some man to come along and fix it for her. It's sad that we women grow up believing in these fairy tales and then are crushed when they turn out not to pertain to real life. In the actual world, we must concern ourselves with our personal growth. Then we'll be able to stand the wait until we encounter a man who is both special and, in Annette's term, "appropriate."

AVOIDING THE LOSER TRACK

And what are the telltale feelings that let you know you're on the loser track with an "inappropriate" man? They are relief that you're no longer alone, leading to gratitude that he's selected you and panic when he's out of your sight. These are difficult feelings to admit to because they make very conscious and concrete our fears of life, adulthood, responsibility, and autonomy. However, such fears are normal and natural. Everybody has experienced them to some degree throughout her life. But remember, the quality, satisfaction, and meaning you get out of your life depends upon how you face those fears. Using an unsatisfactory relationship to camouflage them is a sure way to diminish self-worth.

This thinking was summarized by the therapy patient of mine who coined the term "female escape route," which, as I've said, is a socially acceptable means of avoiding becoming an individual — through attachment.

YOU CAN RUN AWAY FROM YOURSELF, BUT YOU CAN'T HIDE

When she called me, twenty-two-year-old Kristin was a study in panic, hysterical that she'd made an irreversible mistake with her boyfriend of four years. Her problem had begun when the guy, whom she described as "my best friend," announced he was taking an "all-boys" trip during spring break, leaving her, or so it seemed to her, in the lurch.

Consequently, when Kristin and her boyfriend were having dinner at the house of his best friend, along with the other young men with whom he'd be vacationing, she had one drink too many and, in her words, "made a fool of myself." What she'd basically said in no uncertain terms was that if her man couldn't include her in everything he did, she wanted to end the relationship. "And it's kinda true," she told me. "But in the meantime, look what I've done, I'm totally embarrassed and my boy-friend was crying. I just created a big episode and now I don't know how to get out of it."

ATTACHMENT ISN'T INTIMACY

I first suggested that Kristin calm down, then explained that everybody loses it at one time or another. The important thing is to understand why we lost it. And it seemed to me that Kristin's explosion was indicative that she was taking the female escape route by insisting that she become an attachment to her man. Expecting a boyfriend to provide you with your life is unrealistic and actually unfair, because it's simply not his job. Men are here to share our lives, not to be our lives. It's not a question of having too many expectations; it's really about having too few expectations for yourself.

OVERCOMING FEAR THE REAL-WORLD WAY

What I recommended to Kristin, what I rec-ommend to all women, was to do something, such as taking a class or doing community work, which would provide a sense that her life has a purpose outside herself. By so doing, you discover you're not so scared about life because you're excited about establishing your special place in it. Isn't that preferable to being so dependent that the very idea of solitude strikes fear in your heart?

I suggested to Kristin that a good way to begin becoming her own person was to call her boyfriend, tell him that she'd been concerned enough about the incident to elicit my advice and now was working to have a deeper understanding of her own autonomy, then to simply apologize and tell him, sincerely, to have a good time when he was away.

Kristin was lucky that she'd had to confront the issue of dependence on males at twenty-two instead of forty-seven. In fact, she was on the border of doing something very special at a time when she had so many productive years ahead of her to explore her feelings, desires, and the place she really wanted to carve out for herself in the world.

FEAR OF THE UNKNOWN IS HOW GREAT THINGS START

Imagine people going west in covered wagons. They were scared. They had no idea what they'd find. Imagine the first astronauts of the moon landing. Those pioneers may have been heroes, but I guarantee they had their share of fear of the unknown. It just didn't prevent them from acting. All change, as I've said, is scary, but it's the only route to progress. It might help to think of your fears as stage fright, as you prepare to give an Oscar-winning performance as yourself!

EXPECTING THE IMPOSSIBLE — A NO-WIN GAME

If you're inclined to discount my point of view as full of assumptions, as a personal agenda or bias, I understand. After all, it's unsettling to consider the possibility that most female thrusting toward men and relationships is not because women are making sensible choices. Rather, it's a case of women being driven to attach to men for identity, affirmation, approval, purpose, safety, and security — values that can really only come from within ourselves. When the inevitable disappointment happens, such women complain bitterly that their men have failed them because they don't sustain them just the way they want.

DON'T YOU DARE PICK UP THAT PHONE!

My conversation with Stephanie, twenty, made this truth abundantly clear. She immediately expressed her fear of being alone, which she defined as not being in a relationship. I asked her exactly what she feared would happen if she didn't have a guy.

STEPHANIE: I don't know . . . but this has been going on for years with me; I always seem to overlap my relationships. . . . It's almost like I don't know myself, really. And I think that, like, maybe my identity is through these guys.

DR. LAURA: So you're like some Twilight Zone toy. If someone's holding you, you're animated. If they put you down and leave the room, you become an inanimate object. No wonder you race to make sure you've always got a guy around as sort of a battery — they literally give you life.

STEPHANIE: Yes. And security.

DR. LAURA: Oh yeah? What security? You've gone from guy to guy — how secure is that? That's called an "illusion," honey.

STEPHANIE: But I don't want to be like that . . . I want to . . . take care of *me* for a while.

DR. LAURA: "Take care of me," I like that — that's well put.

STEPHANIE: I say it, but doing it . . . It seems that when I end a relationship . . .

DR. LAURA: You get right back on the guy-patrol alert?

STEPHANIE: I try to stop myself . . .

DR. LAURA: The same way it's hard to say no to a piece of cheesecake, right? . . . So how *are* you going to say no? When the agony of simply being with yourself, utterly devoid of a sense of importance or joy, makes you want to snort, shoot up, or ingest a guy — because that's what it's like, a drug, right?

STEPHANIE: Yes. It takes everything in me to keep from picking up the phone and calling a boyfriend.

DR. LAURA: And that's the very moment you have to keep from doing it. You know where self-esteem ultimately comes from? Surviving that painful moment and not picking up the phone. Not by seducing some new guy — but by suffering through the pain. And, Stephanie, you *do* have the personal courage it takes — you've just been too afraid to test it!

FIVE RIGHT THINGS TO DO WHEN YOU'RE DRIVEN TO DO A WRONG ONE

What Stephanie needed was a game plan to combat those "dark nights of the soul." She needed to tell herself, "When I get scared, whether it's expressed as boredom, loneliness, feeling lost, or as if I have no meaning in my life and no direction, at that moment, I'll pull out my list of five good things to do, out of which I'll choose one or more." These things will enable women to get past that horrendous moment of self-doubting fear — and avoid "eating the cheesecake."

Those five things could include calling a friend who knows and understands you and your situation, someone who can give you "first refusal." The list may include taking a bath or a walk, writing in a journal, exercising, meditating, having a cup of hot tea — anything that puts some time and energy between the "impulse to act" and the actual choice to action.

60

Usually, if some centering behavior intercedes, the pain can be survived and you are on to new planes of your own growing existence.

MAKING A MAN THE JUDGE AND JURY OF YOUR SELF-WORTH

Men are not only seen and used by many women as a place to hide from the difficulties and discomforts of becoming an autonomous human being, as we've seen thus far. They are often burdened with the task of being the source of affirmation and approval for the woman's young, uncertain, developing, or even somewhat damaged self-esteem.

If she can make him stay, she's okay. If he leaves, she's not okay. To attribute such godlike powers to someone you just happen to meet in the unpredictable "crapshoot" of life is, in a word, stupid. And remember, that kind of stupidity has nothing to do with I.Q. because it's a universal truth that some of the smartest women do the stupidest things.

WHAT IF I DO SOMETHING WRONG AND RUIN IT?

Emily, a twenty-year-old college student majoring in childhood education, professed to be very happy in her ten month relationship with a twenty-seven-year-old. And yet when she called me, she was crying. When I asked her the problem, she blurted out that she was constantly terrified that she was going to do something wrong and ruin it.

I asked her if she was equally afraid that he might do something wrong and ruin it and she emphatically replied no, but, under my prodding, she soon admitted that he could get a job out of state and leave. She told me plaintively, "He could say that I am not worth it, too young or something, or not mature enough to handle it." I agreed that some of that might be true but suggested that what she was really afraid of was slipping up and showing him what she really is.

THE SMART PART

Before long, Emily was confessing to her fears of not being smart enough to achieve her goal of being a kindergarten and preschool teacher. She claimed to be both dedicated and perseverant; it was the smart part that set off her worry attacks. "People don't have confidence in me," she insisted, and when I demanded a specific example, she immediately responded, "My family."

DR. LAURA: Who in your family doesn't have confidence in you?
EMILY: My mother.
DR. LAURA: How do you know that? What does she say?

62

EMILY (CRYING HARDER): . . . Ohhh, I never talked to anybody like this before . . . um . . . she tells me that, you know, when I started school, that "You're not going to finish it" . . .

DR. LAURA: Go ahead, what else did she say?

EMILY (CRYING): That I'm like all my other sisters — that I'm stupid, undependable, irresponsible — but I'm not! Nothing I can say or do . . . Excuse me, I have to calm down.

DR. LAURA: I believe you're not those things — now, why do you think she would say those things if you're not?

EMILY: She can be very abusive, verbally.

DR. LAURA: Has she accomplished anything in her life?

EMILY: No.

DR. LAURA: Oh, now, how do you think that might relate to her tearing down everybody else?

EMILY: Because she feels jealousy for me. There's times she's told me, like when I go somewhere with my friend, "Why should I let you go when I never got to do that when I was your age?" And I go, "Mother, this is a different time . . ."

DR. LAURA: It's just irrelevant. You first have to know that your mother needs a lot of help.

EMILY: Yeah, she does.

DR. LAURA: Now, you may know that, but you are separating what you know intellectually from how you feel — and you feel too often like your mom is right — after all, she is your mom — while in reality you're just a young person with the normal inherent insecurities.

KNOWING IS NOT ALWAYS BELIEVING

At this point, I explained to Emily the nature of the deeper issue: She knew in her mind that her mom was jealous, a bit twisted, and even cruel; but too often she felt that her mom was right. After all, she *was* her mother, so by definition was supposed to know best. And everybody has perfectly normal periods of self-doubt. If you put these factors together, you have a desperately hurt and frightened young lady, whose core fear was that her boyfriend would have the same reaction to her as her mother did. Riddled with such insecurity and dependency, she runs the risk of becoming a pain to her man — unless she begins to work out her emotional conflicts in therapy.

MAKING MEN INTO BAND-AID SOLUTIONS

Everybody's got emotional baggage and idiosyncrasies — that's just real life. For women to expect men to be the bandage for their hurt is to surrender the opportunity to be co-equal and confident in a relationship. Women have work to do before they're ready to make a healthy choice and then to function in a relationship as a healthy partner.

I sometimes feel it should be a felony to marry before thirty. Why? Because women would then be "forced" to take the time to become self-knowledgeable and self-reliant. Then dating would not seem like such a life-and-death necessity. Decisions and choices made out of desperation generally lose you more ground than they can ever gain for you.

CHOOSE OR LOSE

You don't have to be a radical feminist to believe women should make choices. I just don't believe enough of it is happening. One of my aims in writing this book, which I can't stress too often, is that women are hooking onto men by default — with "I love him" becoming the great liberator from personal growth and self-responsibility. In addition, it's not really fair to the man himself, whom you're settling for.

DON'T GET CAUGHT IN THE "VICTIM TRAP"

Probably the single most familiar theme uttered and written by and about women in the popular media is "victimization," replete with graphic stories of dysfunctional this and alcoholic that, so that women are supported to experience interminable "recovery" from terrible pasts. I admit to having a problem with this approach.

Each human being has a story, and the traumas and betrayals are real. Each individual responds to these realities in his or her own unique way. We are not simple formulas of cause and effect. The quality of our lives ultimately depends upon the courage we extend to deal with hurt and risk in a creative way: That is the road to ever growing self-esteem.

And those challenges are available at every age.

CAN "WEDDING JITTERS" BE A WARNING TO GET OUT?

Stacy, my twenty-one-year-old caller, and her thirty-one-year-old live-out boyfriend became engaged five months after they met. Until the engagement began, things had been wonderful, but afterward, Stacy started noticing certain behavior in her Prince Charming. He had become increasingly jealous, controlling, and possessive. At this point, Stacy had had it but was still uncertain if she was doing the right thing by leaving him.

I told Stacy she was doing the right thing unless she wanted to have a life with someone who is perpetually jealous, controlling, and possessive. Then I brought up my theory of the first eighteen months of a relationship's life.

LET'S DECLARE A WAITING PERIOD FOR MARRIAGE

I wholeheartedly believe you should date for about a year and a half before even contemplating engagement. It takes that long to get a clear picture of the other person. Stacy had gotten engaged too soon, before she got that clarification. When you become engaged too quickly, when you've got the ring and announced to the world that you're getting married and then you begin seeing things about your fiancé that are totally unacceptable, it's profoundly embarrassing to do what you know you need to do, which is to get out — at any cost.

FACING REALITY: THE KEY TO GROWTH

Stacy quickly admitted she hadn't really wanted to get engaged in the first place but that the man had insisted on it. Here she was, a nineteen-year-old living in a free country who, because she didn't yet have the strength of her own convictions, bowed to the greater will of an insecure bully who most probably chose a much younger woman so he could order around someone weaker.

YOU'VE GOT TO LEARN TO TRUST YOURSELF

I advised Stacy that the chances of her fiancé changing were slight to nonexistent, as she must by now have surmised, and that what she should do, what she really wanted to do, was gather her courage, take the ring off her finger, give it back to him, and say, "This is too controlling. I have a life I want to develop first. I cannot cater to your fears and your insecurities."

What was clear to me, and what I hope became clear to Stacy, is that she knew what she wanted to do before she called me. In her words, she just "needed to hear it from somebody else." Honestly, what she needed most of all was to learn to trust herself, to hear it from her own mind and accept that it's the right move and go on and live it. That's part and parcel of being a grown-up.

A MAN'S-EYE VIEW OF THE DATING GAME

Now, women, let's take a moment out and explore dating from the guy's point of view. Do you think men are so emotionally dense that they can't sense the difference between your really wanting them and desperately needing attachment? Well, they can! And some of these men, like Stacy's boyfriend, use it to bolster their own insecurity. Too often that sort of situation can become abusive as the controlling aspects of the relationship increase — perhaps in response to the woman's evolving maturity and independence as manifested by her desire to split up.

MEN CAN FEEL LIKE OBJECTS, TOO

Let's not forget that many men are sensitive to our attachment desperation and don't feel wanted for themselves but instead are aware they're being used.

Tony, twenty-nine, had been dating a certain woman for almost a year. He was in therapy in order to deal with his own intimacy problems but was growing increasingly dismayed by the behavior of his girlfriend. She would always look at him with goo-goo eyes and extol the perfection of the relationship even though he was not reciprocating on anything even remotely close to her level. Despite her extraordinary devotion, she never seemed interested in what he was really feeling or thinking. Maybe, he suggested, she didn't want to confront a truth that might interfere with her fantasy.

TONY: I don't understand. I go, "How could you want to be with someone who is not giving you back what you're giving?" And she basically said at the end of the conversation,

"Look, I'm tired of being the suffering female . . ."

DR. LAURA: Good, I'm glad she is.

TONY: So she said that and that was fine. But she's still calling me and suffering and saying she doesn't understand why she is in so much pain, she didn't do anything to earn it, and so on. Like last night she just moved into a new apartment and it was raining, you know that's kind of creepy stuff, so she called me . . . real late . . . terrified . . .

DR. LAURA: Clearly, she's trying to make you feel responsible for her and suck you back in. And you don't even describe her as wanting an intimate relationship with you. You describe her as wanting a RELATIONSHIP — in capital letters. But she can't have it by telling you it's perfect or that she's scared in her apartment, because it's not you she is really learning anything about — thoughts, feelings, needs — it's just you as a generic man, date, or boyfriend. Am I right?

TONY: A thousand percent.

THERE AIN'T NOTHING LIKE THE REAL THING

No one will deny the enormous ego gratification involved in having someone attracted to you. There is pleasure in having a good time with somebody. There is comfort in having somebody share many of your perspectives. Affirmation, approval, and attachment are beneficial and wonderful aspects of relationships. The excitement of all those feelings coming together is exhilarating. And they are some of the many benefits of relating to other human beings.

If you are desperate for affirmation, approval, and attachment, if you're grateful to be chosen, so you're not too choosy, if you are settling instead of being selective, then you are probably making stupid dating choices. Think about it: Would the kind of man you really want want a gal who behaves like you? No.

On January 7, 1993, Suzanne, thirty, called me, all confused about whether or not she should continue to date her thirty-two-year-old boyfriend of three months. It seems that when his mother comes to town she stays at his house. Well, it's more than that. She sleeps with him in his bed.

"He says that they don't 'do' anything," she whimpered. "So I asked him why his mom doesn't just sleep in another bed in his house. He answered me back by saying I'm too conservative.

"Is this okay? I just don't know if I should date him anymore. Am I overreacting?"

Need I say more?

3. Stupid Devotion

"BUT I LOVE HIM" AND MORE STUPID ROMANTIC STUFF

You cannot imagine how frustrating it is to hear over and over "I love him" as the justification for a bad choice in a man. These women can't face the fact that they're immobilized in an obviously self-defeating situation, gratefully tolerating attitudes and behaviors no man would give quarter to for five seconds. Their definition of love is — with a lot of confirmation from popular culture — way off the mark and has become synonymous with attachment.

WHOEVER SAID SURRENDER IS ROMANTIC HAD A MAJOR PROBLEM

Let's look briefly at current popular role models for women in love as personified by contemporary fairy tales, which all our children know by heart.

Ariel, the Little Mermaid, aspires to "greater things" and ends up with a stupid prince, who "loved whoever had that 'voice,'" no matter how wonderful Ariel was. For this, she gives up her world, her family, her fins.

Belle, in *Beauty and the Beast*, aspires to "greater things" and ends up with a rotten (oh, maybe he'll change . . .) prince who at first worked on being nice to her only to break a curse. Okay, okay, so he came around — but would Prince Handsome have hung around that long for a witch? I hardly think so. For this she gave up her plans and dreams of journeying into the world.

I would have been happier had she been a part of his successful spiritual transformation, patted him on the head, and gave him her forwarding address at the university.

In *Aladdin*, the princess also gives up her dreams of venturing into the world, independently, when her beggar-turned-prince takes her off on a magic carpet. He's going to show her the world — of course, that he's never seen it himself is irrelevant.

If you're thinking these "fairy tales" do not apply to real life, think again! Remember, billions of girls and boys who see these films are going to grow up believing this romantic nonsense and dreaming dreams that could later turn into nightmares.

DREAMS CAN BE DANGEROUS

Since we're on the subject of dreams, I want to point out the crucial difference between really caring for someone in particular and caring desperately for the dream. By caring more for the dream, by being dependent upon making an attachment, women make compromises that can destroy them. Consider Lisa's story:

COME GET ME, CONVINCE ME, SHOW ME YOU LOVE ME!

Lisa described herself as "kind of in a predicament right now," which turned out to be the understatement of the week. She had been dating a man for a year and a half (my recommended minimum waiting period for marriage), and he had recently proposed to her. Having taken the time to get clarification, she told him no because of his many problems, which included drug use and abusive behavior.

Although she claimed her boyfriend was trying to curb his temper and hadn't pushed her around for three months, Lisa was still concerned because that last abuse had taken place when she had tried to break off the relationship.

DR. LAURA: Lisa, what the heck are you doing there?

LISA: I don't know. I really have been trying to get out . . . but I can't get rid of him. I'll refuse to take his phone calls or answer the door — anything — and he'll still come over or he'll bust through the door. . . .

DR. LAURA: Then you call the police.

LISA: I haven't had the heart . . .

DR. LAURA: The heart! Lisa, what he is doing is against the law. Breaking and entering and stalking are crimes!

LISA: But sometimes he can be —

DR. LAURA: Sometimes, nothing! Lisa. I'm going to sound very harsh for a moment. You cannot afford to be a wimpy, overcompassionate, frightened female, because you'll be putting yourself in real physical danger. You need to take the appropriate steps to protect yourself and let him know you are not playing a dramatic love game of "come get me — convince me — make me know you love me — when I say no." Can you do that?

LISA: Yesss . . .

DR. LAURA: You must convince him you're really serious when you say, "Go away." Even if he's nice from time to time. Even if he gets down on his knees and swears he'll try to change. I just don't think an abusive, intrusive drug addict is a good father for your children-to-be. Do you think so?

LISA: No . . . but is it natural to still feel like I love him?

DR. LAURA: Perhaps you're feeling for your dream, for those moments when it's pleasant. Unfortunately, a relationship is not about moment-to-moment. It's about totality. What you have to do is stand back and not look at any one moment. You have to say, "Overall, this is a really bad choice," and get the heck out!

LISA: Okay, thank you.

NO MORE MS. NICE GAL!

Although Lisa can clearly see this man is a major problem, she continues to have feelings for him. So what's really at issue? That's extremely complicated, but here's at least a partial explanation.

We all know the phrase "a face only a mother could love." Therein lies a clue to solving the mystery. I can't tell you precisely what combination of nature and nurture is at work here, but women do seem able (and all too willing) to search really hard for redeeming qualities in their men. With such a mind-set, they are ripe to be overly tolerant of grossly negative qualities in exchange for what may be only moments of happiness or peace.

THE DETESTABLE DOUBLE STANDARD

I'm reminded of the Ann Landers column in which a woman was complaining about how difficult it was for a "quality lady over thirty-five" to find a "nice guy": "I find it fascinating," she wrote, "that women are willing to overlook balding heads, beer bellies and plaid shirts with polka-dot ties, but a man will take me aside and whisper, 'She's okay but she has thighs in two different time zones.' "

And think of all those beer commercials in which the guys are schleppy but their dream women have to be at least in the running for the cover of the *Sports Illustrated* swimsuit issue. Are we, as "normal" women, expected not only to be satisfied with such jerks but deeply gratified when they deign to favor us with their attention?

SELECT, DON'T SETTLE

Unfortunately, women's willingness to overlook troubling traits doesn't stop at schleppiness. It includes, for instance, drug and alcohol problems, abusiveness, immaturity, irresponsibility — and more.

Much too much more.

And all in order to settle for fantasy versions of love, commitment, security, attachment, identity, and purpose.

Why are you settling? Why are you not more selective? Why are you not more critical?

Why are you calling it love?

Because you haven't come to believe in yourself!

And when you don't believe in yourself, you find yourself believing in things considerably more foolish than the Tooth Fairy.

WHY DO WOMEN PUT UP WITH BAD-NEWS BOORS?

Suzanne had been seeing her boyfriend for six months when he broke the news that he was moving back with his ex-wife — for three months, for financial reasons. To add insult to injury, she subsequently discovered he was still married to the woman, although they'd been separated for seven years, and had a seven-year-old son by her.

After meeting the wife, Suzanne realized the "divorce" was only the tip of an iceberg of dishonesty: The entire time he'd been romancing her, even suggesting they marry, the man had been sleeping with his wife. As far as the other woman knew, there were no financial reasons and no three-month time limit on his living with her; they were simply getting back together. When Suzanne confronted the louse, he not only denied everything, but he made her feel as if *she* were the one with the problem. Then came this shocking statement:

"BUT I . . . I STILL JUST . . . REALLY LOVE HIM."

When I suggested to Suzanne that she was probably dealing with a sociopath — a master at manipulating women who were made vulnerable by self-doubt into assuming guilt — she didn't disagree. When she told me he had been

78

in AA for over a year, she listened with interest as I countered, "So what, Suzanne. I don't care what he's been in or for how long. The most adequate measure of the man is what he does when he's not in meetings." When she confessed she knew he'd cheated on his wife with at least five other women and I groused, she told me, "I've heard it from everybody, but I needed to hear it from a professional, I guess."

DR. LAURA: Suzanne, this is a bad person, a liar and manipulator. Why aren't you angry and horrified and disgusted enough to make this decision on your own?

SUZANNE: I guess because of my upbringing. A lot of manipulation — but never really lying . . . yeah . . . lying too.

DR. LAURA: So all this is normal to you. You're going to have to struggle against that "normal" so that your new normal is a healthier one. Because he is going to wine, dine, and send you flowers and try to get you back. But people like that don't change. Ask his wife how much he's changed over two decades. Ask yourself how much your family's changed.

SUZANNE: Right, you're right. . . . But is there anything I can do so I don't go back to him? Because — I'm in AA, so I have a support group, but I'm still really scared . . .

DR. LAURA: You have to use your courage. There's no magic here. AA isn't going to give

79

you the courage. And I'm not going to give you the courage. Nothing and nobody has your power to do what you need to do.

SUZANNE (QUIETLY): Yeah.

DR. LAURA: It's up to you, kiddo. You want to have something beautiful and meaningful in your life; you have to hold out for it and in your own mind become the receptacle for it.

SUZANNE (LONG PAUSE WITH SIGHS): I still can't believe I thought he was a good person.

DR. LAURA: You wanted to believe it because he said things you so wanted to hear. He made you feel ways you so badly wanted to feel that you didn't care who he was, really. I can almost still hear it in your voice now. You want too much not to care who he is even now. It's just his wife — right? She's a bitch — we get rid of her and everything will be swell?

SUZANNE: Yeah, I mean, no . . . I really like her!

DR. LAURA: Good, then go out with her instead!

SUZANNE: Really! Thank you so much.

DENIAL GETS YOU NOTHING

If you kiss a toad, you don't get a prince — you get slime in your mouth and bad memories. You do everything but accept reality: You deny, ignore, rationalize, justify, and ultimately go back to that most pathetic defensive position: "But I love him."

What's that supposed to mean, anyway? "I love him," therefore your rational sensibilities are suspended? Now, that's stupid!

THE "BUT I LOVE HIM" FOLLIES

When my caller Jody pleaded, "But I love him . . . ," I suggested that her idea of love — from what she'd described to me — had gotten her into trouble so many times before and was getting her into trouble again. My advice was emphatically not to use those feelings she calls love to make a relationship decision. Since they inevitably led her to the wrong decision, she would do better to tough it out now and spare herself the endless anguish she might otherwise be setting herself up for.

THE LOVE STUFF ISN'T A DIVINE DIRECTIVE

Women like Jody must learn that hormones and heart are not necessarily our best leaders. This love stuff is not an omen or divine directive — so stop wallowing in it! If you find your rational sense being overridden by mushy feelings . . . know that you are probably on the wrong track!

Stop with the "Oh, I know he's __ (fill in the blank with *abusive, mean, cold, uncommunicative, negative, bullying, violent, addicted, controlling, workaholic, jealous,* etc.), but I love him." The "I love him" does not erase what came before!

MY ACID TEST FOR GENUINE LOVE

I feel certain that what many women call love, under so many obviously ugly, hurtful, and sometimes downright dangerous situations, is more about passion and promise and fantasies and desperate dependencies and fears about taking on alternatives.

Real love is a long marination of qualities having to do with respect, admiration, appreciation, character, affection, cooperation, honor, and sacrifice. I ask all these "But I love him" women the same question: "If you were a parent, would you introduce this kind of guy — or even this guy — to your daughter?"

Funny how the answer is always an emphatic No!

WHY CAN'T YOU PUT YOURSELF FIRST?

My comeback is then, "Why would you not be as caring about yourself, as rational about yourself, as you'd be about a daughter?"

Why? Why? Why?

What goes through your mind?

• "If he doesn't want me, I'm no good."

- "I'll never find anyone else to tolerate me."
- "I don't want to be alone."
- "It's better than nothing."
- "It's better than I've had."
- "I'm twenty-nine (thirty-nine, forty-nine, fifty-nine — it's always with a "-nine") and it's getting late for me."
- "I don't really think I could find anybody better."
- "Sometimes he's not so bad."
- "I don't know where I'm going in my life anyway."
- "I'm too uncomfortable with my own problems to face them. Trying to help him makes me feel better."
- "Caring for him makes me feel more meaningful."
- "I'm too scared to face unknowns, inside myself or in the world."
- "It's not so bad."
- "It's hard to find people to have fun with."

LOW SELF-ESTEEM IS NO EXCUSE FOR INACTION

All the above sound like self-esteem problems, don't they?

They are, but the entire low-self-esteem issue is particularly complex, since negative self-worth can also serve as a weapon that women wield against themselves. So many times I'll be asking a woman about her often unfortunate

83

choices and impotent participation in her own life's direction, and the reason she'll give me is "Oh well, I guess it's because I have low self-esteem."

Now, while there is no doubt in my mind that the price tag you put on yourself will determine in large part the value of the people and the situations you'll pick and tolerate, I'm more and more concerned about low self-esteem becoming an excuse for inaction in your own behalf in this sense: You don't feel special, or worthy or competent — therefore, you don't dare take risks.

PAST HURTS DON'T EXCUSE PRESENT COWARDICE

So what do you do when you're feeling consistently down about yourself? You probably search for the childhood hurts that landed you in this pickle, then join an "Adult Child of Whatever" group to give validation to your helplessness. The information you glean and the support you get from self-help books and groups and/or from therapy should help you fight through those reflexive, emotionally induced self-defeating behaviors and choices and to take risks, not linger in negativity.

For it is in the taking of risks, especially in the face of emotional motivations to the contrary, that you grow in autonomy and personal power.

84

Remember, self-esteem is not simply a product of the existence or lack of verbal, emotional, or physical abuse. There are many, many people walking around with positive self-images and expansive worldviews in spite of their terrible upbringings. So the equation between past trauma and low self-esteem can't be one-to-one. I'm not denying the negative impact of early family crises, disruption, or destructiveness. History is not destiny. You have free will to overcome, grow, change: Invent yourself.

WHICH COMES FIRST, COURAGE OR POSITIVE SELF-ESTEEM?

The concept of courage is one I hear discussed almost only when watching *Rescue 911*, but courage is crucial to building, or repairing, a self-image or identity.

Here's my point: Life, with its risks and challenges, is scary. Just as we often turn to instant gratification instead of a more mature postponement of pleasure for some future gain, we often turn too quickly to mechanisms of instant avoidance to deflect risk of failure or hurt.

So, which comes first? Low self-esteem or the absence of an independent, creative effort in life? As with the time-honored "chicken or egg" riddle, which comes first is irrelevant. A lack of self-esteem and a lack of courageous, independent, creative effort on your own behalf will reinforce each other — forever. I suspect this dual failure of the will becomes a self-perpetuating bad habit.

SELF-WORTH:
THE GIFT YOU HAVE TO EARN

If you wait for good self-esteem to set in before you take on life, we'll probably share rocking chairs together as we talk over what might have been.

Your actions often have to come before the feelings, maybe even despite them. As I said before, courage is not the lack of fear, it is fear plus action. You must begin thinking of self-esteem and rational behavior as a continuous loop, each perpetually feeding the other.

THERAPY IS HEALTHY,
DESPERATE ATTACHMENT IS NOT

You are ultimately the architect of your life. Some raw materials might have been left out — or damaged along the way — but you are still the architect of your own life.

So when you examine the blueprints of your relationship, do you — honestly — see a sturdy building or a house of cards? The ultimate quality of your existence will depend upon your exercising the courage to make rational decisions about your relationships early on. That means you'll have to cope with real and irrational feelings of self-doubt and meaninglessness directly, through therapy, for example, rather than indirectly, through desperate attachment.

Otherwise, what you'll call loving feelings are really desperate cries for significance. The loss of that so-called love becomes more than a personal loss — it becomes a person loss: you! And that is the pain thirty-six-year-old Linda was suffering.

HOW TO SURVIVE THE LOSS OF AN ATTACHMENT

Linda was involved with another woman, a twenty-four-year-old, who had informed her that she didn't love Linda and wanted to see other people. But Linda was finding herself unable to let go. I pointed out to her that the issue really was not one of letting go of her lover but of not being able to hold on to herself! There is, after all, a big difference between being hurt and disappointed that someone has rejected you — since we have all been rejected — and making the leap to "I'm worthless and unlovable," which was the tack Linda was taking.

CONNECTING VS. ATTACHING

As the conversation proceeded and Linda admitted she had a tendency to make all her intimate relationships the center of her universe, I observed that such behavior is typically female.

Men don't feel they have to be attached to a woman in order to exist. They feel they have to be doing something: racing a car faster, inventing something, climbing a mountain, running a company — doing something in the world. That's how they find an identity. Women tend not to do that enough. Linda certainly didn't.

DON'T EXPECT MOTIVATION TO FALL FROM THE SKY

"So one of the things you should be working out in therapy," I advised her, "is the evolution, in your original family perhaps, of your discouragement in being independent and autonomous. Second, you'll have to get off your *tush* and have the courage to create something in this world that you can look at and be proud of. And don't expect motivation to fall from the sky. At this point, the motivation will probably have to come from rational thinking. And the rational thought is: If I don't do this, I will always feel this pain."

Dependent women acquire the self-esteem they lack through their attachments to other people. It's a foolhardy means of building self-esteem. Claiming as love the attachment to anyone who barely shows a hint of approval is a desperate state of being. You worry that any minute change in that person's demeanor or behavior might mean his or her lack of interest

— and the loss of you. It makes life a fragile experience.

It is just this kind of state of mind that leads women to look for potential in all the wrong places, and to have the following laments:

LEONORA: I'm kinda hurt and disappointed. I met a guy at work and I've been dating him one month and it's clear that he drinks a lot. What do you think is his potential?

DR. LAURA: Potential for what? Drunk-driving arrests?

DEBBY: I met a man three months ago — we've had a few dates. I found out he's been involved in a shooting. Should I stay?

DR. LAURA: Only after watching *Bonnie and Clyde* for wardrobe suggestions.

LINDA: Well, he has a tendency to lie — actually, he lies a lot. But he is good at other things, if you get what I'm saying. So, what do you think?

DR. LAURA: What "hooks you in"? Does his potency increase in proportion to his lies? Will you really be satisfied with a highly sexed Pinocchio?

DENISE: I'm twenty-eight and I've been dating him for five years. We're engaged for two months. I don't know why, but I still don't trust him. He is irresponsible with money and has been with other women. But he says he loves me. Should I trust him?

DR. LAURA: Why, yes! You should trust that he'll probably be consistently untrustworthy. Which is great if you're not into surprises.

SELLING YOURSELF TO THE LOWEST BIDDER

Can you believe it? These are typical questions! It's not as though the woman has known the man for years and he's recently had a life crisis to which he's responding poorly. These ugly situations generally show themselves in their true light quite early in a relationship. Instead of saying to yourself, "Uh-oh, this is a definite no-no," you act out of a compulsion to grab what's available and make it work no matter what. You too often sell yourself to the available (and usually the lowest) bidder.

GRASPING FOR HOPE MEANS RISKING DESPAIR

A listener letter that can truly be described as heartbreaking illustrates this point perfectly. In it, the writer described her "relationship" with an instructor at an institution that doesn't allow fraternization with students. If the relationship were discovered, the man would be immediately dismissed. "I wonder why he would risk so much to be with me if for only a friendship," the letter continued.

It is most romantic to interpret his "fraternization" as some sort of sacrifice because of his deep feelings for the woman. Unfortunately, what seems more likely is that the teacher is both unethical and self-serving. But that jolt of reality wouldn't fulfill the writer's fantasy, hope, and need. Especially in light of her next disclosure: "I should add that the place where he works has provided me with a great deal of pleasure and friendship since the suicide of my son and subsequent death of my husband."

THE HIGH RISK OF CARING FOR THE DREAM

I can't even imagine the depth of pain, loss, perhaps guilt, fear, and need this woman is experiencing. Her grasping for the hope becomes more understandable. And more perilous. Because too often we only know what we want or need to know.

There is a world of difference between really caring for someone and caring for the dream — of frantically needing the dream as an emotional Band-Aid. If you care for the dream, you don't end up really healing or growing. You just end up hurting from a different source. If ignoring, denial, and rationalization don't work to make this relationship fit — why, become a chameleon. Make yourself fit — at all costs:

THE "VOLUNTEER" HOSTAGE CRISIS

Becky, thirty-six, is with a man who drinks, is verbally abusive, physically violent, owns guns, and now has job problems. How is that for a formula for disaster? "But," she says, "as long as I make things okay — take care of things the way he likes — then it's okay." It is? I don't think so. I think Becky is a volunteer hostage — making the best of what could literally become a life-and-death situation.

IT'S A TERRIBLE FOLLY, TRYING TO FIT

More than just trying to make things okay by appeasing the demons (those guys you just looooooove), so many of you turn yourselves inside out to make your man happy. If he's happy, then you're happy and all is well in the world. Because if he's happy, he'll be nice to you and love you and keep you happily ever after. Right? Wrong! Here's an outstanding example:

RETURNING TO THE SCENE OF THE CRIME

Twenty-year-old Valerie had been going with a young man about her age for more than two years. The relationship was troubled, and Valerie decided to fix it by changing herself to

92

fit his ideals and trying to do everything he wanted of her. Unfortunately, the tactics hadn't worked. Her man was still discontented. At this point, she had had it, but every time she tried to end the affair, she was so overwhelmed with loneliness that she inevitably went back.

When I asked her why she kept "returning to the scene of the crime," she pleaded ignorance, then told me, "I guess it's because I miss him." Miss him? The source of perpetual negative judgment and rejection — plus some sex and handholding? For this she continued to give up pieces of herself?

I suggested that she was losing too many pieces of herself for so little positive return from this insecure, immature, controlling young man.

WHEN YOU'RE REENACTING OLD PAIN

I was particularly curious as to why Valerie was giving a youth with little more experience than she the power to define her. Under further scrutiny, the reason became clear. Valerie was the product of a broken home. She had a reservoir of unresolved emotions about the disappearance of her dad when she was only six. Now she was acting them out by being utterly submissive for fear that she, like her mother, would "do something wrong" and chase the man away, thereby losing "Daddy" again.

By the time our conversation concluded, Valerie seemed ready to unload the boyfriend, since they both needed time to grow, to face the fact that she was reenacting past pain, frustration, hurt, and loss and to begin to accept her own lovability and start exploring her own desires and dreams.

ROMANTIC INSTANT REPLAY

Valerie's predicament exemplifies behavior I encounter frequently: using the new love as a replacement part for an old loss — usually of a parent. It's not, therefore, the new guy who is the real target of your lovin' feelings. It is what he symbolizes, what he gives you a second chance to resolve. That's why his eventual loss becomes so devastating: It is an instant replay of a primal hurt!

WHY WOMEN AVOID NEW CHALLENGES — WITH ALL THEIR MIGHT

There are two powerful motivations for making it work with the most available guy — attempting to heal past hurts and avoiding risks. Sadly, neither works for long — even if a romance takes off and you're swept away by passion. When reality steps in, you go back to reading EMPTY and start trying to figure out why you're still not happy. Nine times out of ten, you come up with the following solution: Some change has to be made in him! Then everything will be okay.

RESISTANCE TO RISK-TAKING AND LOW SELF-ESTEEM — THE DEADLY DUO

Diane, forty-two, has a boyfriend whom she describes as self-centered. "He is always putting me down and discounting me," she complains. "We have fights about this all the time. I keep trying to get him to understand and to change."

I ask Diane what the benefits are to struggling to make him change. She answers, "Number one, I don't have to change.

"Number two, I don't lose what I like in the companionship and security aspects.

"Number three, it would be uncomfortable making a transition to being alone or with anyone else.

"And number four, I guess, I would take it personally — his negative perceptions of me must be right."

Wow! How is that for self-knowledge and honesty! We're back to those same old bugaboos: resistance to risk-taking and low self-esteem — hereafter to be known as "the deadly duo."

THE FATAL "BUT . . ."

Want another sure indicator that you're on the wrong track? It's when, after you admit to knowing what you're doing is probably stupid, you add anything reminiscent of the word *but*. Oh, I know, but, maybe, what if . . . ! Honey, you can't afford to live in the land of "what if." Because you — and I and everyone else — are living in the land of what is. Take up residence, please, and look at the buts as what they are, last-ditch attempts to struggle against the inevitable next step: personal growth.

HOW DO I TEACH HIM TO RESPECT ME?

Don't think you're going to trip me up on the compassion or pity issue! Elizabeth writes, "I can't take the insults anymore! They're hurtful and I never know why he gets mad till it's too late. Help! How do I teach him to respect me?" And I respond, "By doing what any truly self-respecting person would do under those circumstances: Leave. That will provide the most profound lesson he can learn from you!"

ARE YOU A ROMANTIC MARTYR?

Barbara complains, "My boyfriend and I have been dating for over a year. So far, there has been no intimacy and almost no touching.

He doesn't like to be touched, or so he says. It's easy to understand why, with his background. His father was very abusive to him, his mother, five sisters, including beatings and sexual abuse . . ." And I answer, "This is a fella I would suggest you refer to a good therapist and forget. If you feel inexorably drawn in such 'what if' directions, we need to talk about your anxieties about intimacy — because the bottom line is that when you are with a guy who can't/won't do it, you're not doing it. And just maybe, that's they way you like it — safe from confronting your inner demons by martyring yourself to his."

GIVING IS NO GUARANTEE OF GETTING ANYTHING BACK

Remember that when your identity depends on becoming indispensable, you'll collect a lot of takers, but the chances are you will not often find that caretaking returned. You get something by communicating need, by being open to the gift but not, not ever, by settling.

CHANGING HIM FOR YOUR OWN GOOD

When women attempt to attain value and definition by attachment to men, a strange thing happens: They become vigilant to any imperfections in him — because if he's not perfect, then, by association, neither are they. That's when you try to fix him for your own good. Of course, this will be registered by him as behavior that is castrating, bitchy, unloving, and unaccepting. So it rarely results in any change coming from him, because he isn't the one motivated for the changes — you are. Unfortunately, you aren't exercising the option of change in the person who really needs it: you.

JUST HOW MUCH POINTLESS PAIN CAN YOU TAKE?

It's amazing how much nonproductive anguish and suffering (abuse, mismatch, disdain, disinterest) women will endure in order to avoid the productive forms of anguish and suffering (inner knowledge, independence, and challenging life for a personal dream). I stress again: No genuine, fulfilling love is possible without self-love preceding it.

THE AGE-OLD HEART VS. HEAD DEBATE

To sum up, please don't mix up feelings comprised of familiarity, investment, sex, promises, hopes, and fantasies with love. If those are the feelings tugging at your heart strings, forget it!

I'm asked all the time about whether decisions in relationships should be made from the head or the heart. You can guess my answer — the head, always. Because the heart is notorious for having a more blurry picture of reality.

And you know, when it comes to a long-term, committed relationship: Love is not enough. There are issues of honor, respect, mutuality, sacrifice, acceptance, supportiveness, similarity of life values and morality, to name only a few. They, too, don't come without struggling and striving, but, oh, are they worth it!

P.S.: IS THIS WOMAN FOR REAL?

Believe it or not, dear reader, this is a genuine news story, which the Associated Press released on March 9, 1993:

A woman whose husband is accused of poisoning her and killing two others with cyanide-tainted cold capsules says she considers their relationship normal even though she once dialed 911 seeking help during a fight.

Joseph Meling is charged with six counts of product tampering, two counts of perjury, and three counts of insurance fraud. He is accused of putting a cyanide capsule into a Sudafed package in February 1991 to kill his wife for $700,000 in life insurance. He also is accused of tampering with five Sudafed packages in stores to make it appear a random killer was at work.

Kathleen Daneker, 40, of Tacoma and Stan McWhorter, 44, of Lacey died of cyanide poisoning from Sudafed purchased around Tacoma and Olympia. Three other cyanide-filled capsules were found in Sudafed packages during a recall of the product.

Mrs. Meling nearly died but eventually recovered. She filed divorce papers soon after the cyanide incident, but later went back to her husband and is testifying in his defense.

Mrs. Meling said she felt the conflict in her marriage was normal. At times in tears, Mrs. Meling said she still loves Meling, and believes he is innocent.

Go figure!

4. Stupid Passion

"OHHH, AHHH, WE'RE BREATHING HARD. . . . IT MUST MEAN LOVE"

I remember a series of commercials some years ago in which Orson Welles intoned: "We will sell no wine before its time." Would that more women would display the same attitude toward sex!

And please don't accuse me of being a throwback to the double-standard days without considering the increasing numbers of unwanted pregnancies, abortions, venereal diseases, and broken hearts since the sexual revolution told us: "Hey, baby, you have the same right to fun 'n' games as men do."

I agree we've come a long way, dahlin', but we're still not where we want to be — because women continue to overromanticize sex.

IS ONE NIGHT OF HEAVEN WORTH THE AFTERMATH FROM HELL?

This from Ellen, who called in during my stint filling in for Sally Jessy Raphael on her ABC Radio Network show: "I'm a secretary who's been in love with my boss for a year. I never actually said anything about it to him. He never acted any way but businesslike with me.

"A month ago he asked me out to dinner on a Friday night. Then we went to his house to have some wine and talk, and I ended up staying the weekend. It was great. The sex was fantastic — it was all so romantic — just like a dream come true. We didn't talk about what would happen now at the office, or anything, before I went home on Sunday night. Okay. It's been over three weeks now and he treats me exactly like he did before that weekend! He hasn't said a word. My feelings are very hurt and I don't know what to do. I feel very uncomfortable."

HOPE EQUALS RESIGNATION

Find me a woman who can't relate to that caller's hurt and embarrassment — leading back to the old-fashioned now-comic question "But will he respect me in the morning?" That's yet another of our fatal buts. Still, the issue isn't really his respect. The issue is how we women can fantasize that something is so without bothering to question or discuss it. We hold our breath and hope it all turns out okay. Listen: In the words of Nobel Prize winner Albert Camus, "Hope equals resignation, and to live is not to resign yourself."

When I asked Ellen her thoughts on being sexual with her boss without a prior discussion about the relationship, she replied, "I thought that if he had sex with me, it meant that he feels like I do."

So there it is: relationship by hopeful fantasy.

THE VIRGIN-TILL-DEATH ACT

Let me repeat, this is not an issue of his respect — the old double standard. And I am not saying women should do a virgin-till-death act to make a man see them as pure, good, or a prize to be won. That would produce the desired effect only with a man who has an inferiority complex. However, a man who is heavily indoctrinated in a fundamentalist mentality would require a mate in kind — perhaps a better plan than the sexual chaos we have now.

BEWARE THE DON JUANS OF THIS WORLD!

Let's face it, it's perfectly possible to have a complete discussion with a man who seems to be on the same wavelength only to find out he is a liar, that he is someone playing a game with others. It happens. It always has. It always will. Remember Don Juan (whose real problem was his mother, of course . . .)? I'm sorry to report he's alive and well and living practically everywhere. Finally, I'm much more concerned with you playing games with yourselves — expecting pleasure while you're actually setting yourselves up for pain.

I FEEL LIKE I BETRAYED MY FRIEND!

That is what my caller Tiffany did to herself, all the while trying to believe things were more substantial than was actually the case. She came on the air telling me she was "having a lot of problems dealing with a mistake I made." The "mistake" turned out to be getting sexually involved with a very close friend's husband. (She herself was unmarried.)

Now, she regretted it tremendously, wished it had never taken place. Although it had only happened once some five weeks earlier, it plagued her. When I asked Tiffany why she'd done it in the first place, she initially claimed she didn't know, and then . . .

TIFFANY: Well, he sort of approached me about it and, um, what is killing me the most is that he approached me and I responded. And I don't know exactly why . . . except . . . I thought that I needed to help him, in a way . . . because his wife . . . my friend . . . had just died two weeks before and now I . . . I feel like I betrayed her . . . like she's going, "Why did you do this to me?"

DR. LAURA: You didn't do this to her. You obviously have done something to hurt yourself. Do you like this man? Did you have warmies for him when she was alive?

TIFFANY: I don't think so. . . . Well . . . yes and no . . . yes.

DR. LAURA: So you already coveted him in your heart. And now there was the opportunity — but now you feel uncomfortable about it because he's pulled back a bit?

TIFFANY: Yeah, me also. It was sort of a mutual thing.

DR. LAURA: Okay, would you say he pulled back a little before you pulled back? Might that be what hurts and makes you feel so bad at this point?

TIFFANY: Yes.

DR. LAURA: I think you're feeling a little used. What might be helpful is to verbalize all this to him.

TIFFANY: Well, we haven't been talking to each other at all.

DR. LAURA: Even so, I still prescribe calling him and talking it out — and, even if it makes you blush, facing it directly, matter-of-factly. Say something like "I've always been fond of you, you came on to me, and I thought I could be there for you at this time of pain . . . and now it feels like I just got used." Tell him you understand it was a mutual experience. But that what you have to do right now is pull back.

TIFFANY: Oh, I don't know if I can do that . . .

DR. LAURA: Consider the alternative. Is it easier to just sit there and obsess on how you betrayed a friend? And you didn't even do that!

TIFFANY: Yeah, okay.

DR. LAURA: And, Tiffany, if he comes on to you again, don't go with the flow until you are more certain — with the passing months or maybe years — that he's dealt with his wife's death and is really available for another relationship. Okay? Now, you take care.

TIFFANY: Thank you. Thanks a lot.

INTIMACY AND SEXUALITY ARE NOT THE SAME THING

Both men and women call me to talk about their relationships. Both use the term *intimate* to imply they've had sex. So does that mean intimacy and sexuality are synonymous? Absolutely not!

Within one hour from right now you could be having frenzied sex with a complete stranger. This is obviously not intimacy. Intimacy is not the ability to do it — fruit flies can do it. Intimacy is the ability to talk over the doing of it — and everything else, from the meaning of sex to the meaning of life.

I have often said on the air, "Don't do anything you can't talk about — with that person!"

TALK NOW, SEX LATER

So why don't you talk first and have sex later? Well, first, there is a tremendous vulnerability associated with self-expression: the pain of anticipated rejection or criticism. A caller, when questioned about why she won't ask her fella of one month if he is dating other women, replies, "I don't want to be upset by the answer."

"But," I counter, "you are already upset by the worrying and wondering if he is or not!"

"Yeah, I know," she explains, "but the upset is in my head. If I know for sure, then it's real hurt."

SHOULD I CALL HIM — OR WAIT TILL HE CALLS ME?

Here's an example of how unarticulated fantasizing works — or, rather, doesn't work:

Diana, a single parent who'd been divorced for two years, had a certain need, a human need, the need to be connected to another human being, to be cared about, to touch and to feel close. In the course of things, she'd struck up a renewed friendship with a man she'd known as a teenager.

The relationship initially consisted of his doing odd jobs around the house when she needed male help — until the night her children were away, and she invited him over for dinner "to thank him." Thanking him consisted of sleeping with him. And she hadn't heard from him since — although she freely admitted she was the one who had been doing the calling all along.

SEXUALIZING INSTEAD OF ROMANTICIZING

When Diana used the term *romantic* to describe their encounter, I pointed out that to men, sex doesn't necessarily include romance — although, since we women tend to put them together in our minds, we assume our partner does too. In Diana's case, the reality was that a situation had been sexualized, not romanticized. At least, not for him.

DIANA: Right. So I don't know if I should just leave it and not call again or call him and clear the air or . . .

DR. LAURA: When you say "clear the air," what might you say? Because you need to be real clear about the message you want to give him. He may think you're getting serious now that you two have had sex — and he may not want that responsibility.

DIANA: Uh-huh. Yeah. Yeah.

DR. LAURA: So you need clarity. To be mad at him isn't fair because you didn't ever say, "Let's have a discussion about our relationship and what sex will mean for you." You guys didn't agree to anything. It just happened.

DIANA: Yeah, part of me is mad about that — but I needed, I guess, the nurturing. It's been a long, long time. And it felt good at the time, and he did say, "You'll be hearing from me" before he left, then I thought, "Oh, what did I do?" And a month has gone by and I've been patiently waiting — because I didn't want to seem like I'm chasing him. And I haven't heard anything.

DR. LAURA: Well, Diana, that is your answer.

DIANA: Yeah. But I don't know if I should . . .

DR. LAURA: When you say, "I don't know if I should . . . ," it's as though you mean, "If I make this phone call, I'll still have this nurturing support system." What you really have to adjust to is that you don't.

DIANA: It was really nice when we were just friends.

DR. LAURA: You know, Diana, I think women have to cut out the romantic fantasy and talk turkey before they get into bed. Because if we don't clarify what it is we're doing before we do it, we can't complain about being misunderstood or used.

DIANA: But, right now, what do you think I should do? Never call him, or just wait for him to call me?

DR. LAURA: You might call to talk or leave a message on his machine saying, "I don't want to lose what was a friendship by over-romanticizing what was a very nice but clearly a sexual evening. I'd still like you to come over from time to time, without any commitment and responsibility." And I would hope he would respect that amount of chutzpah. But, Diana, don't make that call

109

unless that is exactly what you mean. Otherwise, you are just manipulating.

DIANA: Yeah, okay. That sounds good to me. Thanks so much.

SEEING ONLY WHAT
YOU WANT TO SEE

That Diana's friend did odd jobs for her and ate her meals gave her hope. That he never called or showed initiative in any more personal way she ignored. Sex, she figured incorrectly, would make it be okay. As in Diana's case, sex too often happens too soon because it is used to satisfy loneliness or starvation for approval.

THE SEXUAL VICIOUS CIRCLE

Maria, nineteen, called to say, "I'm having sex with this guy who has said plainly that he doesn't love me and that he doesn't want to marry me. I don't know why, but I don't stop seeing him and having sex with him. He's older. I guess I keep thinking that he must love me if he has sex with me. But then, I know it's not true."

Maria told me she never felt love from her parents and that the only moments she thought she'd ever experienced as love were those sexual moments. It was just too much to give up. And so, the vicious circle: not feeling loved or lovable — having sex to feel love — realizing

110

later that it was sex and not love — not feeling loved or lovable, etc. The catastrophe here is that the current reality of her behavior perpetually reinforces an assumed notion of herself as unlovable.

STOP GROVELING FOR AFFECTION!

I stressed to Maria that children are inherently lovable. And if parents don't love, it's because they can't love — they are the ones who are broken. I also pointed out that her desperate attachment to this man was actually retarding her development toward being able to love.

"Maria," I concluded, "all of your energies are directed toward getting what you interpret as affection or approval. Be careful you don't find yourself living a life that way; never giving, never growing — just always trying to harvest empty fields."

EXPLODING THE MYTH OF SEX AS AN ANTIDOTE FOR LONELINESS

Sex never works as a hoped-for cure or anesthesia for feelings of inadequacy, emptiness, shame, loneliness, fearfulness, self-disgust, and more. Oh, that it had that much power! I have worked with so many women, educated and successful or not, who have used a man's sexual interest and approval as a means of buoying a sinking feeling of worthlessness. The problem is that it just doesn't work for longer than the moment — if that.

WAKING UP WITH A STRANGER
YOU CAN'T STAND

Caroline, a private patient, was in her late thirties and recently divorced from a fellow who, according to her, was extraordinarily handsome but congenitally immature. Although attractive, extremely bright, creative, and talented, she was not as pretty as her ex. She was an artsy type while her family were all lawyers. She was tall and gangly and didn't really seem to fit in. It wasn't that her family didn't love and support her — they did. It was just that she still felt very "unattractive and weird" because of the difference she perceived between herself and them.

Caroline's prototypical relationship was getting sexually passionate immediately, then waking up the next morning feeling uninterested in or disgusted by — the guy. Any man she stayed with for more than a night was inevitably an offbeat type with whom she felt more comfortable.

THERE ARE SUCCESS STORIES!

When the pain of this pattern just got too great, Caroline turned to therapy to work on it. I'm happy to report that as a result of treat-

112

ment, she became closer to her family and more sanguine about herself. The rule we established for her was: When you meet a new guy, no sex for six weeks (for her, an eternity!). She kept to it — allowing time for a relationship of communication and some vulnerability to be established before plunging between the sheets.

In Caroline's case, the pattern of sex-too-soon served the purpose of making her feeling accepted and in control; she rejected first, saving herself from anticipated rejection.

DARE TO PUT YOUR NEGATIVE SELF-IMAGE TO THE TEST

Another patient of mine, Martha, muses aloud, "I feel that sex is the only thing I really have going for me. What would a guy be attracted to me for without that? How would I keep him?"

I suggest we put her supposition to the test. Martha goes back to school as a means of building self-esteem and does great. Now she experiments with men differently: She spends time with them to see if she's right — that is, if without sex no one will be interested in her. To her amazement, she discovers she's wrong. This reality checking takes courage, but then, so does everything else worth having in life.

SEXUAL PASSION VS. MATURE LOVE

Sexual passion is a consuming feeling. You can't think, work, sleep, or do anything without the distraction of a tidal wave of visceral emotion. Mature love puts sexual passion in a context and perspective that is less all-consuming. For some women, that reality is disappointing because they're left with themselves — unmasked again.

WHEN THE THRILL GOES

Twenty-five-year-old Monica called to say, "I've been in a relationship for almost three years now, and sexually it was very good for the first year or so. When it was good, the sex was very satisfying for both of us. I felt very sexy and very free to be myself with him and I had a really good time." Then, about a year and a half into the relationship, Monica noticed that "for some reason something was freezing" her sexually.

When I pushed her, she admitted the reason: She wasn't feeling comfortable with herself because, although she had always been conscious of her figure, she'd begun gaining weight — at the same time that her sexual drive began to diminish. Under my urging, she admitted that she thought the weight gain was the result of her no longer going to a gym. And that was provoked by her unhappiness with her job, which wasn't — and never had been — fulfilling.

DR. LAURA: So you were never doing your dream.

MONICA: Exactly!

DR. LAURA: What is your dream?

MONICA: To work with animals. I'd like to go work for the zoo.

DR. LAURA: So why didn't you go do that?

MONICA: Well, I just think they wouldn't want me.

DR. LAURA: Who? The animals?

MONICA: No, the people who would interview me.

DR. LAURA: Well, you had to interview to get the job you have now. What about you would turn them off?

MONICA: Maybe that I'm not skilled enough.

DR. LAURA: Of course you're not! You've got to learn it. So you were unhappy with yourself and with your life and you found this boyfriend who made you feel great and you had the infatuation. And frankly, those feelings took you away from all the bad stuff. But those feelings only lasted so long and now you are back confronting Monica. This is not about sex. This is about your impotency in your own life!

MONICA: That's interesting.

DR. LAURA: So, what you may want to do is go put on some decent clothes — the army boots they wear when they march around the

115

zoo — call up, make an appointment, and go get a job, however menial. And learn all you can and work your way up to your dream. And that's okay. It's called "experience" and it's a blessing, not a curse. Because when you work toward your dream and away from the ache, you'll stop using sex as a painkiller.

MONICA: Wow! I thought there was something wrong with me sexually.

DR. LAURA: The only thing wrong with you is that you quit on your dream! That's what's wrong with you, woman! Go for it, Monica. This is your one life. Go for it!

MONICA: That's great. Thank you for the encouragement!

BUT I CAN'T HELP MYSELF — I'M SEXUALLY ADDICTED

Monica expected sexual passion to carry her through the rest of her life. But that only works if every year you get a new guy and start out with infatuation all over again. Many people do that and then call it a disease: "I'm sexually addicted."

But I say you are not sick — all you are doing is trying to get a high instead of dealing with personal empowerment and self-control. Monica's in for a pleasant surprise: the tremendous and lasting high of going for the interview, and the second one, and saying, "Please, I'll do anything, I'll sweep up after the elephants, just

116

give me a chance to work here."

Many women, like Monica, hope or expect that sexual passion or love will carry them through their lives, without their going for their dreams. They're dead wrong.

THE SHOCKING ADMISSION THAT IT'S ALL UP TO YOU

Some women who have sex-too-soon in their lives figure it out:

Lisa, twenty-two, began our conversation by telling me she'd left her husband a year earlier. She'd been married at eighteen, right out of high school, because of an unplanned pregnancy. She was now the mother of a three-year-old son. At that time, she had no plans for the future outside of being an ideal wife and mother. Describing herself as "not the school type," she admitted that as a teen, she was totally "boy crazy," then surprised me by explaining that behavior with a great deal of clarity. "I just wanted a boyfriend to make me feel good about myself. I had very low self-esteem, so I always had a boyfriend . . . always . . . and this guy was 'wanted' by everyone. And I got him."

"So," I said, "this marriage didn't really have to do with love, it had more to do with filling what felt empty." She agreed, then proceeded to describe the genuine fulfillment of motherhood and added, "And I'm working on my own," something of which her ex had told her she was incapable.

THE PROFOUND SATISFACTION OF INDEPENDENCE

Lisa's ex-husband had merely echoed her own fears. He would tell her, "You'll never do anything!" Now she found herself in the enviable position of knowing they were both wrong. Even the hassle of trying to perform well at work and be there for her adored son twenty-four hours a day was a source of satisfaction because she was doing it by herself. She'd even been dating a lot, but so far had found nobody worthwhile. When she laughingly told me, "My ex isn't bad, I'm just not attracted to him anymore," I replied, "You know, you really didn't get married out of love — and he wasn't supportive of your growth — a foundation for true loving. You got married out of desperation. You were sexual even before that out of desperation — emotional desperation. That's not love. So I'm not surprised you're not attracted to him any more."

ACKNOWLEDGING THAT A MISTAKE IS NEVER A MISTAKE

My advice to Lisa was to acknowledge the fact that her marriage had been a mistake and continue moving on with her life. As far as having a man was concerned, I suggested that her son might, for the moment, be the only male she needed. Lisa seemed to know instinctively that the only person who could provide her with a feeling of self-worth was . . . herself. In closing, I told her, "Start dreaming about twenty years from now — I'd like a call from you when you've got a dream — it doesn't necessarily have to come to pass. The dreams I've had have changed. But it's important that you dream. Because if you can dream for your future, it means you believe in yourself now."

DON'T OVERLOOK YOUR OWN GROWTH

Lisa was figuring it all out but didn't realize and appreciate her own growth. I was thrilled to be able to point it out to her. Which shows you how much we all need objective feedback and a good support system. Our inner changes happen so slowly that we sometimes don't see them — we're too into survival mode.

"SEX-TOO-SOON" CAN BECOME A LIFE SENTENCE

The consequences of engaging in sexual relationships before a woman is ready (in her head, her heart, and her life) are quite serious. And sometimes quite complex and emotionally disastrous.

Karen's voice, when I took her call, clued me in at once that she was upset — and angry. But she started blandly enough by telling me she was in a three-year live-in relationship with "a gentleman." Then she said she was twenty (uh-oh!) and — here's the kicker — that they had an eight-month-old baby together. Although she assured me that she and the father were engaged to be married, she dropped another bomb when she added, "And I just found out yesterday that he has another child, a newborn, by an ex-girlfriend." Suggesting that her guy (I couldn't bear to call him her "gentleman") liked to keep his options open, I asked if he'd actually agreed to a wedding date. Of course, he hadn't.

"So I'm dying to hear your question," I told her.

"I'm just not sure what to do," she answered.

SEXUAL INTIMACY RARELY LEADS TO INSTANT COMMITMENT

My response was to tell her that wasn't accurate. She was sure what to do — or what she would have done if she wasn't locked into a seemingly no-win situation. "If you had been going with this guy for a bit and had a job with a future and no kid," I said, "I bet you'd tell him to leave." She agreed. I pointed out he didn't sound like a good bet for a lifelong partner in any case; it was Karen's romantic notion

120

that sexual intimacy leads to instant commitment that had blurred her judgment about him all along.

Since rushing into things she wasn't ready for had caused her present difficulties, I advised Karen not to marry anybody for several years and to stop living with her so-called fiancé. Over the cooling-off period, while they remained civil and worked at parenting their baby, Karen would see if the guy was capable of the loving monogamy she desired as well as fulfilling his complicated obligations to both his children.

"The best thing you can do," I reiterated in closing, "is to give yourself these two years before making a decision — even if you have to fight the urge to marry or dump him. That's a very small percentage of time to make a decision that will affect a significant amount of your life."

AS LONG AS YOU'RE ALIVE, YOU HAVE CHOICES

Karen's relief was so apparent I realized she hadn't even considered the possibility that she had choices. My heart goes out to young women like her, struggling through what ought to be the freest time of their lives. As with pregnant teenagers, women in general refuse to read the handwriting on the wall until they are compelled to by the sheer weight of the graffiti

121

bringing the whole wall down. Then, in such sad ways, it's often too late.

THE YOUNGER THE WOMAN, THE GREATER THE FANTASY

Just yesterday, an angry father called my program wondering how to punish his sixteen-year-old daughter for having lost her virginity. He'd learned this from the girl's grandmother, who accidently (how do you do that?) read her diary. I told him that a week without Nintendo probably wouldn't have the impact he hoped for and that the discussion had to be more profound than that and called for greater sensitivity and understanding on his part. I don't think he heard me — but I'd like to share what I tried to explain to him with you:

Once sex, especially sex-too-soon, enters a young woman's relationship with a man, she perceives the affair to be a far more meaningful situation than it probably would be without the physical intimacy.

As a woman caller said, "I made a mistake early by becoming sexually involved before knowing more about this person. From that point on, because we were intimately connected 'in that sense,' I feel like I'm kind of stuck."

This perception is all the more magnified by young people's lack of integrated identity and life experiences, and their greater dependency needs.

122

IS THERE A RIGHT AGE TO BEGIN BEING SEXUAL?

During an appearance on the now defunct Ron Reagan TV show, I was badgered by Mr. Reagan to give an exact "age" at which kids should begin to have sex. My answer, obviously unsatisfactory to his TV talk-show format, was that we shouldn't engage in activities until we are mature enough to comprehend, anticipate, and accept the possible consequences of the behaviors. To give a universal age would be possible only if everyone alive matured at the same rate and, in fact, had an identical nature. That they don't is the crux of the problem.

Ovaries, testes, penises, vaginas, and uteri are in operational status long before the individuals housing them have the wisdom and maturity to be responsible for the consequences: pregnancy or venereal disease or emotional pain from this disappointment of counting on sex to be not only the "glue" in the relationship but the saving grace in a frightened life. But sex-too-soon doesn't only happen to teenagers . . .

SEX-TOO-SOON IS SELF-LOVE-TOO-LATE

Hilda, twenty-five, commenting on getting into a sexual relationship immediately, says, "I want it all at once to hide who I am." Sex-too-soon is self-love-too-late.

Carolyn, thirty-three, realizes that.

Carolyn has a three-year-old son, the product of a one-night stand with a neighborhood fellow. She says, "I knew at the time it wasn't right. I just went ahead and did it anyway."

"Why?" I ask, rather bluntly.

"Well, quite honestly," she responds, "I was lonely, overweight, not too many suitors, no sex since sixteen years old, and was feeling isolated, having just recently moved into a new house in a new neighborhood. All in all, it felt good at the time."

"And now?" I asked.

"Now, I've got a wonderful little boy, whom I love dearly, but who's got no daddy."

The emotional vacuum of Carolyn's life obviously gave birth to an impulsive act, which gave birth to a son.

ULTIMATELY, THE ISSUE IS SELF-ESTEEM

Joan, forty-two, was wondering about even calling the man in question a boyfriend, since, after only four weeks in a relationship, he'd dumped her two weeks before, claiming he wanted a looser relationship, without requirements or commitments. In other words, he was willing to have "fun and chuckles," aka sex, with her, but didn't want a relationship.

"On the one hand," she lamented, "I'm going to miss the sex. On the other hand, it's not good for my self-esteem."

So I asked her, "Which one is more important?"

"Well," she replied, "at certain times of the month . . . the sex!"

We both laughed at that! Still, Joan's is a typical female pattern: I want to feel good. I want to feel secure. I want to be loved and cherished. I want it all right now. Therefore, I'll have sex now. That will ensure me the rest. Then I can complain to my girlfriends and him about how he's hurting me.

WHAT SEX-TOO-SOON CAN DO TO YOU

Before we move on, I want to stress this: No matter what your age is, sex — a powerful experience and driving force — doesn't have the power to validate you or your relationship. It's actually the other way around. Sex-too-soon can end up making you feel even more self-denigrated, desperate — and terribly alone.

5. Stupid Cohabitation

THE ULTIMATE FEMALE SELF-DELUSION

When I began working on radio some fifteen years ago, it was rare for a caller to admit she was shacking up with a guy. There seems to have been a relaxation of values and norms. Today, living-in no longer has a stigma attached to it.

The conventional wisdom in favor of living-in before marriage is that it allows the couple to get to know each other, make a better marital choice, and lay a more solid conjugal foundation than men and women who marry cold turkey.

Could this thinking be wrong?

IS LIVING-IN THE KISS OF DEATH TO A RELATIONSHIP?

According to psychologist David G. Myers, Ph.D., author of *The Pursuit of Happiness*, seven recent studies concur that couples who cohabit with their spouses-to-be have a higher divorce rate than those who don't. Three national surveys illustrate this: A U.S. survey of 13,000

126

adults found that couples who lived together before marriage were one-third more likely to separate or divorce within a decade. A Canadian national survey of 5,300 women found that those who cohabited were 54 percent more likely to divorce within fifteen years. And a Swedish study of 4,300 women found cohabitation linked with an 80 percent greater risk of divorce.

WHY PLAY RUSSIAN ROULETTE WITH YOUR LIFE?

Now, you and I both know how easy it is to discount all that data! You simply say, "But my situation is different."

Well, for some of you, that's true! There are those successful transitions. It happens. But it is not the rule. So why are you willing, even eager, to play Russian roulette with your life? Why? Desperation. Fear of not having somebody — of not having a life if a man doesn't want you.

In our dialogues you always come to admit it. How about saving yourself the stress of finding it out the hard way?

Perhaps waiting and growing in maturity, independence, and security-of-self are too tough to do — especially when you are young and needy and hoping to escape an unhappy past.

I LOVE HIM, BUT
I JUST DON'T TRUST HIM . . .

Jessica, a nineteen-year-old aspiring dancer, came from a troubled family in which her father had played around. Her upbringing had provided her with very little security and an exaggerated inability to trust. Despite that, she had been living with her boyfriend for four months and claimed she was in love with him, although she had trouble believing in his caring and fidelity. In her words, she was "hoping for something beautiful," i.e., marriage, as proof of his caring.

I pointed out to Jessica that she was very insecure and that part of what often makes very young women move in with a man early is their hope that by association (preferably marriage) with the fellow, they will feel better about themselves and about life. And you know something? It never, never works that way.

LIVING-IN AS A RETARDANT
TO MATURITY

Jessica's primary job is to build her self-esteem and competency, so that when she chooses somebody, it isn't out of a desperate need to heal the hurts of the past. It should be out of a desire to share herself, her life's experience. And that's why, in the long run, I don't think personal maturity is benefited by these living-in arrangements especially at Jessica's age and with her history of loss and betrayal.

WHEN HOPE CAN HURT YOU

There are exceptions to everything in life, infinite combinations and permutations to experience. For the most part, living-in is usually entered into, as Jessica did, with fantasy and hopefulness and an agenda that isn't even admitted to the self. Look at Jessica's "wanting something beautiful." There is almost inevitably the vain hope that being with a man will make something magical happen.

And Jessica's not alone in that. Everybody fantasizes at some time about bypassing the hard work of growing up and growing stronger.

But nobody can — not if they want to find some fulfillment in this life. When Jessica does the work and learns to take care of herself, she won't have to hope for something beautiful. She'll be creating it.

ONLY YOU CAN MAKE YOU HAPPY

Listen, the phrase is "happily ever after." All of us girls grew up with that promise. So when you're an unhappy young girl, what better remedy than living-in with a man? The problem is that happiness just isn't won that easily — and it's not a matter of who *you* are with but who *he* is with (i.e., you!).

You and only you have the power, the sole power, to make you happy. When you blindly leap for a man, you generally end up repeating, reliving, the pain you've been trying to flee. That's why Jessica is agonizing over not being able to trust her man no matter what her instinct tells her.

DENIAL AND LIVING-IN

Denial is a big factor in this living-in arrangement. And the styles of that denial — as you'll see in the course of this chapter — run the gamut from denial of one's own true needs and wants to denial of what he is about.

One quote from a caller named Jane highlights the latter: "I feel he does love me, but he holds back" is her explanation for the live-in boyfriend's desire to sex-swap with other couples. Sadly, she goes on to say, "I might do that for him if I knew how we stood . . ."

IF HE REALLY LOVED ME, WOULDN'T HE MARRY ME?

Moving in with a man when you don't know how he feels is to try to make him feel something toward you. That's demeaning and stupid. It is about you auditioning.

Diana knew that. She and her boyfriend had been together for over a year and had been living together for five months. Although she claimed they constantly talked about marriage, a truer version would be that the "they" was really her. Her lover responded to her entreaties by saying he wanted to marry her but he didn't know when because he didn't "feel ready."

DIANA: Should I stick around and wait? It could be five or six years . . .

DR. LAURA: Diana, are you sure you're reading him right? He may not want to marry you. We can't really interpret what he means when he says he is not ready. But we can see why you put yourself in this frustrating situation. You are living-in to audition, hoping to get the part of the bride. Am I right?

DIANA: Ummm . . . yeah.

DR. LAURA: But you haven't, which means it wasn't a good plan. Look, he is content. You're anything but. You are motivated for something to change, he is not. Contented people are not motivated to make changes. Do you agree?

DIANA: Yeah.

DR. LAURA: So you're the one who's going to have to make the changes. Get out of there! Date him. If you like him, date him!

DIANA: Well, that's what we've been talking about lately.

DR. LAURA: Sounds sensible.

DIANA: He also said he'd go into therapy with me and talk about it.

DR. LAURA: That's nice, too. But right now I'm not interested in him. I'm concerned about you. Diana, leave. Leave because living with him is making you feel bad about yourself. That's why you shouldn't be there. It is damaging to you. Promise me you'll think about what I've said.

DIANA: Absolutely. And thanks. I really needed to hear that.

DR. LAURA: Take care — and move!

LIVING-IN IS NO PROOF OF GROWTH

All through this call, I had a feeling that Diana's relationship had solid potential but needed more space and time to grow. Moving in together seems to imply that this growth process has already happened. Then, when things don't fall into place as the woman thinks they should, she gets all bent out of shape.

WHAT AM I STILL DOING HERE IF HE DOESN'T WANT ME?

Jean, thirty, a part-time student with an independent income, had been living rent-free with her boyfriend for a year and a half. Prior to that, she'd been separated from her now ex-husband and hadn't been meeting many men. When she connected with her present guy and they became close, she thought, Well, this seems to feel good. "So we became closer, and

I moved in." At this point, I couldn't figure out why she'd called.

As she talked, the reality of her situation became increasingly upsetting. Although Jean had no children, the man's seventeen- and thirteen-year-olds were living with them, but the father was adamant — sometimes almost violent — about Jean keeping her distance from them.

"What does that mean?" I asked her. "You're not supposed to talk to them? Give them orders?"

"He doesn't want me to participate in their lives at all," she replied. "He always tells me, 'I just want you to take care of me. Don't worry about them.' "

I still wasn't absolutely certain why Jean had called — until she mentioned that her man "goes through spells" when he wants her to leave, then relents. When she added, "I try to convince him that we have so much going for each other," I told her, "You can't convince somebody of that. They are the measure of what they think and feel. Having that argument is a waste of time and demeaning to you."

JEAN: Yes, but I keep saying to myself, "This is the move I need to do, to leave. What am I doing here if he doesn't want me?"

DR. LAURA: Notice how you don't ask yourself if you really want to be with him. Oh, I'm sure he wants you there. I'm sure he likes the sex, and you sound like a nice lady . . .

JEAN: I try to make everybody happy.

DR. LAURA: What about you, Jean? Are you making yourself happy? Is he making you happy? . . . Can I be blunt?

JEAN: Yes, please.

DR. LAURA: This arrangement is very demeaning to you. You have no long-term commitment from him, yet he has made it clear what your position is — to service him. When he feels like it, he even seems to get some pleasure from making you feel insecure. And you know why you put up with it? Because you're too scared to be on your own. You're grateful to be owned because it relieves you of responsibility.

JEAN: Is that why I don't leave? Because I'm scared to take responsibility?

DR. LAURA: Right. You let your fear have all the power. Jean, you sold out. You see, he is taking care of you in some ways — such as financially. But you are not taking care of yourself.

JEAN: Exactly. And that has to change.

DR. LAURA: Exactly. Jean, take care — of yourself!

LIVING-IN = GIVING IN

Women, remember, self-esteem is centered in the will to overcome circumstance, not to give in to being overcome. As in Jean's case, the

134

giving in often takes the form of living-in. The results may be twofold: a roof over the head — and a sinkhole under the heart. Women have to know of their alternatives to selling themselves. And they have to be able to use their courage and creativity in ways that make them choosers, not beggars.

DON'T EVER SETTLE FOR LESS

Women ask me quite often how to get a man to respect them, to treat them with respect. My answer is always the same: Never settle for or permit less. If he can't rise to that occasion, dump him. Conversions only come from within. But some women just don't seem to get that message. They just keep hopin' and tryin', like Yolanda.

I THOUGHT I WAS IN
A MONOGAMOUS RELATIONSHIP!

Yolanda, a thirty-eight-year-old social-services technician, called to discuss the fact that her live-in boyfriend of three years had admitted to spending the weekend with another woman. She was horrified that her fantasies of a monogamous relationship were dashed now that she knew he was fooling around.

I pointed out to Yolanda that when you move in with a man without a commitment, he already knows one crucial thing: He doesn't have

135

to do much to get you. Then he fools around, and you stay, and he learns something more: He doesn't have to do much to keep you, either. And that has to be crushing to your self-respect.

Yolanda came across as a nice person, educated, a professional, who meant something in the world. I urged her to hold out for the right man, a man who would make a commitment to her, and added that she wasn't going to find one while she was frittering away her time — out of desperation — with a man who didn't seem to respect her or to be interested in pleasing her — only himself. She was clearly furious at him and disillusioned and had the financial means to move out. I only hope she had the emotional ones as well.

MAKE NO MISTAKE, COMMITMENT *IS* A BIG DEAL

Now, you might well argue: "Big deal, a commitment. Commitments don't stop people from being abusive, unloving, unfaithful, or just plain annoying. Commitments don't even stop people from dumping each other. So — big deal."

Well, the statistics prove that commitment is a big deal; as I quoted earlier in this chapter, ". . . compared to couples who don't cohabit with their spouses-to-be, those who do have higher divorce rates."

A SOLID FOUNDATION REQUIRES
TIME, EFFORT, AND SACRIFICE

The interesting question is Why? There are probably many forces at work here, worthy of a book to itself, but I feel strongly that the main contributors are maturity, patience, and the ability to postpone gratification.

When people aren't willing to put in the time and effort to build a foundation, to build something solid and meaningful, they are usually not the ones to persist with effort and sacrifice to develop it and keep it going.

Having sex-too-soon, moving in without commitments or life plans in concert, are the behaviors of basically immature, let-me-feel-good-right-now-because-I-want-it-therefore-it-is kind of people. The immaturity has to do also with not having developed an esteem and identity that permit you to be right out there with the truth of your needs and feelings.

You're scared, so you play it "safe." And then you find out that *safe* doesn't always have the big payoff! That's what my caller Sharon found out.

WHEN YOU WANT A FAMILY
AND HE DOESN'T

Sharon told me she had originally decided to move in with her boyfriend because she wanted "to get to know him better." And in fact, over the course of a couple of years, they had become close. In her words, "It's the ultimate, ideal relationship. He's wonderful to me and I believe I am to him. We are very supportive of each other, have a lot in common, and we enjoy each other's company." So why was she calling?

The problem was that Sharon had moved in without marriage in her mind (consciously, at least), and the subject hadn't been discussed. Now she found herself wanting marriage and a family, but her boyfriend didn't feel he was up to the enhanced responsibilities. And he was emphatic about it. In order not to rock the boat, Sharon seemed willing to put her own desires on the back burner, but I cautioned her that as time passed, she might get increasingly frustrated — and angry at him.

"And that isn't fair," I advised her, "because every step of the way, you made the choices. Like many women, you've been lying to yourself in the hope that the relationship will evolve. That's a calculated risk. If you're able to erase the notion of marriage and babies from your mind, that's one thing. But if you're kidding yourself in order not to lose him, that's a mistake!"

IMMEDIATE LOSSES/
LONG-TERM GAINS

Imagine the choices Sharon is now facing —

agonizing choices: to leave a satisfying relationship or not; to leave someone she loves and enjoys to seek another who will more match what she now dares to dream — marriage and family. The immediate losses are obvious. The long-term gain is unpredictable. Often, when a woman states her intent to jump ship, suddenly the man, not wanting to experience great loss either, decides to start paddling faster.

GOOD DECISIONS REQUIRE OBJECTIVITY

Nonetheless, as we go through life, growing, changing, maturing, this type of crossroads experience is expected, typical, and human. No surprise. That's not the element that concerns me — that's just real life. My concern is that when relationships prematurely take on elements of sexuality and living-in, it makes it more difficult to have the objectivity required to make good decisions.

YOU'RE TOO BUSY MAKING SURE HE WANTS YOU TO QUESTION WHETHER YOU WANT HIM

Women do not move in to check out the guy from closer range. Women move in to be protected, taken care of, to be wanted. And when you are in that mind-set, you can't for a moment wonder (especially not out loud) if

139

you even want the guy — you're too busy making sure he wants you.

Controlling, petty, selfish, insecure, destructive, immature, and hurtful behaviors of the man in question become things to work around rather than qualities to examine to decide on his worthiness to you! It is harder to ask yourself the very important question "Is this how I want to live the rest of my life?" when you are already dug in!

THE MATE MAKEOVER — A STUDY IN SELF-DELUSION

Susan called me to discuss her boyfriend's immature and manipulative behavior, which she was determined to change!

DR. LAURA: You live with him?
SUSAN: Yes.
DR. LAURA: You got sexual too soon. You moved in too soon. You got engaged and you are looking square into your future — and saying "yuk." But instead of making a judgment, you are asking little-girl questions about how you can make him over.
SUSAN: Yeah, I guess so.
DR. LAURA: And that's because once you've established all that you have, it is difficult to imagine backtracking. If you were simply dating, you'd look at his hypersensitivity and immaturity, be turned off, and not date him

140

anymore — because you'd have a whole other life to fall back on. When you commit this much to living together, it makes it extremely hard to do what you need to do. So you use a Band-Aid rather than a scalpel when major surgery is required.

DATING AS A LEASE WITH AN OPTION TO BUY

Dating — not living-in — is supposed to be about learning and discerning. Dating is supposed to be a kind of lease with option — so don't get sexual and cohabit right away and change the meaning of dating to a "lease with premature obligations" situation!

THE RETURN OF THE LIVING DREAD: "BUT I . . ."

Since our dating and love chapters we haven't invoked the old reliable "But he said," as motivation for our stupid choices. Let's do it now.

Dana, a thirty-three-year-old divorcée with two children, called to say she was considering leaving a five-year relationship. She and her kids were living with the boyfriend, who had a problem: He was not divorced. "He's been pretty much back and forth for several years," she told me, "because, I'd say, of guilt. He is very Catholic. I'm not. Maybe that's just an excuse . . . anyway, I feel like I'm coaching him all the time, 'Did you talk to the attorney? Did you talk to the therapist?' "

To make matters worse, his wife wouldn't allow his kids to visit his new household, which meant that any time the fellow spent with them, such as holidays, were awful for Dana and her daughters. "And if he is with us, he might as well not be because he's so depressed," Dana told me. "And in this past year he has done nothing legally to change things."

When I asked her why she moved in to begin with, she responded, "Because he kept telling me everything was going to change. And I . . . I just believed him." To which I countered, "That's like jumping off the end of a swimming pool, saying, 'He told me there would be water in it by the time I hit bottom!' "

YOU DON'T REALLY HAVE A MAN, ANYWAY

This is what I advised Dana: "I think that no matter what he does to straighten himself out, you and the children have got to get your own place and start leading your own lives. That would be a better climate for your kids — first of all, because I don't think the decisions you are making are good for them. I think it would be a step forward from where you are now. Especially in terms of maturity and how to handle

142

grown-up situations of commitment and attachment.

"Dana, he is weak, and you've made it easy for him. You must know by now, it doesn't matter what he promises. Until he has fixed his life and shown some strength and integrity and maturity to handle that appropriately, you don't have much of a man anyway."

I FEEL GREAT ABOUT MOVING IN — EXCEPT FOR THESE NAGGING DOUBTS . . .

Nicole knew I wasn't an advocate of living-in when she called, but she claimed, as many do, "We have a little bit more of a situation than that." Whatever that meant — because when I asked her directly, "Nicole, are you trying to convince yourself to move in?" she responded, "Well, I want to — but there is still a part of me that is hesitating."

DR. LAURA: Listen to that part of you. When you guys are both ready to make that commitment, make it! The indication is that living-in doesn't work if you think it's supposed to help you work on how to be together. And I've got to tell you I think it's a stupid idea. The only reason I would live with somebody is if I didn't want to get married.

NICOLE: Well, I do want to marry him. But he says it's a big step for him.

143

DR. LAURA: Then wait till he's ready to take that step. A commitment is a social statement and an inner promise — if he's not ready, pretending that he is by moving in won't make it so!

NICOLE: I'm trying to compromise.

DR. LAURA: I don't even believe I heard you say that! No compromise, honey. Don't you compromise yourself. If you want to get married and you feel this is the guy, date him, enjoy him, and see if in time you both feel the desire for that commitment. If he doesn't want to get married and you do and you move in to play marriage, you really have compromised — and gained nothing.

NICOLE: I think I knew all this!

DR. LAURA: Well, you certainly knew how I felt about this living-in issue before you called. So maybe you wanted some confirmation. Good for you! And don't back down when he flashes his baby browns at you. Okay?

NICOLE: Okay, thanks.

HE'S THE ONE WHO SHOULD FEEL GUILTY, NOT YOU!

So he says it is a big step for him and she is supposed to feel guilty and greedy for wanting more. Women, don't let yourselves be beguiled and manipulated by that. And don't tolerate the injunction that you are being manipulative.

Grown-ups should know that they don't get the goodies legitimately unless they have earned them. Look out for the word *compromise* if it ends up meaning you give up what is precious to you so that maybe you'll get what you want later.

You will live to regret it — Jackie did!

WHY IS MY LIVE-IN LOVER SEXUALLY HARASSING ME?

Jackie calls to discuss the fact that her live-in boyfriend of three years has begun constantly fondling her breasts — at inappropriate times.

"He only does it at home," she complains, "but it still just drives me crazy. Like, when I'm washing the dishes or just walking by, instead of giving me a hug, he grabs my boobs. When I tell him it bothers me, he goes, 'Fine, I'll never touch you again.' I just don't know how to respond — we get nowhere."

Under my prodding, Jackie admits there was a time when such behavior was mutually pleasing but that something has changed in her attitude, then confesses they've been angry at each other because she wants the relationship to graduate to a level other than just living together. Consequently, she feels annoyed when he takes intimate liberties without reciprocating with what she wants — marriage.

"So," I observe, "this is not about boobs — this is about a commitment. This is about you feeling insulted that you are in the no-win position of being totally available without a reciprocal agreement from him." When she agrees, I urge her to move out. If she wishes, she can continue to see him, making it clear she wants to be married to him but that she doesn't want to start hating him — which she surely will if things continue along their present course.

And Jackie agrees to try to establish some independence for herself.

LIVING TOGETHER AND MATURITY GO HAND IN HAND

To sum up: People have problems. There are no relationships without problems. The issue is whether people have the maturity and the commitment to hang in there with each other and work out the problems. Or do they have the inner strength and courage to admit to a mistake and let go. That's what makes the difference.

A living-in arrangement does not inherently have that kind of commitment; nor is it a further step in that direction. Living-in is more a convenience and a fantasy; typically the former for men, the latter for women. As you've surely guessed by now, I'm very agin' it. Let's get pragmatic: Statistics show that living-in doesn't ensure a quality, long-lasting marriage, probably because the attitude of one of the partners is more "Let's see if this feels good to me every day," and the attitude of the other is "I'll be careful, lest he not feel good about me today." The true tragedy is when the more-available sex brings forth a child into this situation. The child usually ends up the product of a never-was but still-broken home.

LOVE IS ABOUT A LOT MORE THAN PASSION

So, couples have problems. But with maturity, caring, and commitment, they can get through them. Those are the relationships that last and grow into love. Because love isn't instant. It takes years and working through problems together and growth and nurturing each other's growth. That's what grows love, and it involves a lot more than passion. It takes commitment.

P.S.: PARDON A PERSONAL PAT ON THE BACK

On Mother's Day I received this letter from a happy mom: "After listening to you, my twenty-three-year-old daughter opted for marriage instead of their living-in arrangement." And that, as they say, made my day.

6. Stupid Expectations

FIRST YOU COMMIT TO HIM, THEN YOU HATE HIM!?

This query is addressed to every woman who married "the man of her dreams," only to feel as though she's passed through the Twilight Zone into a perpetual nightmare:

Q: Why is it that the very qualities that mesmerized you about him in courtship are now seemingly more repellent than bathing in worms marinated in manure?

A: Simple. You are disappointed. Somehow, the fantasies and the hopes turned threatening.

DID YOU MISREAD THE HANDWRITING ON THE WALL?

Is your disappointment justified? Only when it's a rare case of "bait 'n' switch" — in which your Dr. Jekyll boyfriend metamorphoses into a marital Mr. Hyde.

More typically, women see the handwriting on the wall quite clearly but are later struck down due to their own ancient emotional black holes.

In other words, you picked him because of your own unmet needs and frustrated yearnings. And then you hate him because of your own unmet needs and frustrated yearnings.

How do we make sense out of that?

ARE ALL DISAPPOINTMENTS MISTAKES?

Surprise! The answer is no!

The disappointment may be a great opportunity for personal growth and emotional healing of childhood hurts — if you are ready to assume personal responsibility and endure the discomforts of change.

THE PERILS OF CLINGING TO THE PAST

As a case in point, let me share with you the story of Kenny and Maureen.

Maureen told me she was calling for an appointment out of concern for her sixteen-month-old baby, who was "acting up a lot." Since I already had the notion that the child was Maureen's ticket into therapy, I suggested she also bring her husband to the session. The young couple arrived on time, with an adorable baby in their arms. The "problem" — the infant's chronic upset, crying, nervousness — I recognized quickly as a response to the chronic upset, crying, and nervousness of her mom and dad.

Critical Attraction

Maureen came from a very poor, very unstable southern family, complete with repeatedly vanishing father. A veritable Blanche DuBois, she was childlike in her demeanor, weepy, anxious, and very unhappy. Her main complaints about Kenny concerned his — she was so furious, she couldn't say his name! — coldness, argumentativeness, criticalness, bossiness, and lack of affection.

Kenny, on the other hand, was from an ultrastable, decidedly patriarchal family that gave little quarter or value to any accomplishment that wasn't goal-oriented. He complained about Maureen's overemotionality, flightiness, lack of competency in areas of grown-up responsibility (such as being able to balance a checkbook), and general immaturity.

With the baby on her lap getting more and more restless (subsequent sessions did not include the child), Maureen finally uttered those sad words, "I think I want a divorce."

Attaching to Repair Childhood Hurts

This couple's pain brought into focus for me the underlying, perhaps even unconscious, mechanism we have for attaching to repair early childhood hurts. And don't try to get away with "that stuff is all behind me because I'm a grown-up now." We are all composites of every moment and experience in our lives.

Of course, the meaning and magnitude of the

150

impact of any life experience depends upon our individual interpretation — which depends on our personal vulnerabilities as well as the quality of our support systems and general healthfulness of our emotional environment. In other words, what may be a trauma to you can seem to a friend simply a sad, painful, upsetting life experience to get through in order to go forward.

Dueling Priorities

Through our discussions, it became clear that Kenny's priorities included the work ethic, being responsible, being right. Issues of emotions, spirituality, philosophy, even relationships, he considered "things in the way." He was focusing exclusively on those values that would please his father — no matter how Kenny himself felt or what he needed.

Maureen's priorities were to stay attached and ensure what she saw as security. For her, issues of will, opinion, personal goals, and competency were the "things in the way." She was focusing on avoiding the traumas that had dominated her emotional life since childhood.

What I Told Kenny

"You do not permit yourself to get in touch with your gentler, dependent, needy, emotional self. I'm pretty sure that's because your father didn't admit that this self exists in all of us. He even went so far as to punish you when you did

151

display it. Kenny, do you realize you are mostly leading your life unaware you're still programmed to please your dad?

"Now. You married Maureen because she embodied the fulfillment, reservoir, and expression of those 'taboo' parts of yourself. Why else choose someone you see as having all the parts you disdain? In addition, her apparent weakness makes you feel secure because she so clearly needs you. Once we accept ourselves, Kenny, we don't labor to disavow parts of ourselves, do we?"

What I Told Maureen

"Your personal insecurity is a reaction to the very real and repetitive abandonment and consequent insecurity that marked your childhood. It seems to me that your fear of not having a daddy or even food to eat has made you gear up to make sure your grown-up life would not repeat that pain.

"So you married Mr. Responsible. Now you can tell time by when he comes and goes and what he does, and it's driving you up a wall. And that's because you haven't worked on your own personal growth — and for a very potent reason. Because it leads toward autonomy, while you've been striving for attachment, so that this time you could keep your dad. Well, babe, you wanted a strong fellow you could count on — and you got him."

What I Told Them Both

"Both of you got exactly what you hoped for and needed in a mate. To that extent you picked right! But the original pain out of which this choice was made hasn't been relieved. That is so tremendously disappointing and puzzling that you end up blaming each other as if the pain were new.

"The issue at this point," I concluded, "ought not be how you can divorce each other. It should be how you have divorced important parts of yourselves out of need for a parent. You are adults, and that parental loss (emotional or actual) must be accepted. In so doing, you will take on the more grown-up role of giving and taking with a healthier balance and range of behaviors. Right now both of you are playing only one tiny, perpetual role."

Mutual Support Is Key

I'm happy to report that as the result of our work together, Kenny began to allow Maureen to mother and "lover" him, while Maureen began assuming more responsibility in her own right. They supported each other's measured growth — and were mutually pleased with the results. And, hallelujah, the baby calmed down!

MALE DEPENDENCY:
THE OTHER SIDE OF THE COIN

You must realize that if you are aware of your

low self-esteem and dependency, the man in your life may be, too, but he's probably manifesting it differently. Maureen and Kenny are prime examples of that fact.

Dependent women get weepy and clingy, while dependent men get blustery and controlling. Still, those behaviors are really different sides of the same coin. Since people with low self-esteem tend to seek their own level when pairing up, never feel you're beneath the man you're with, because he's probably your camouflaged match — and has an equal problem!

When Maureen picked Kenny to avoid the hurts of childhood, she relinquished her need for personal growth and power. She thought she hated Kenny because he kept her down. In reality, she traded off being "one down" in exchange for not being one alone. Understandably, she hated what she had become. It is not unusual to deny, ignore, or not understand that you hate yourself — and simply hate him instead.

KNOWING BETTER — AND DOING IT ANYWAY — THIS DISAPPOINTMENT DOES MEAN MISTAKE!

How can you tell if you're getting into one of these no-win situations? It's easy, actually. From discussions I have had with women over the years, I have a distinct impression that you know . . . and do it anyway.

When she called, Lila immediately announced she was in a long-distance relationship. She lived in L.A. while her boyfriend lived in northern California, and they'd been commuting for a year. They were at the point where they had a crucial decision to make: either break up or spend more time together in order to test the solidity of their feelings for each other.

Lila freely admitted she was thirty-eight and tired of being alone, living alone, and being lonely. She had a good professional life and friends, but she felt they weren't adequate substitutes for someone at home and a family. Ultimately, she and her man had decided to live together, which meant Lila would have to relocate. Now she was getting cold feet and starting to experience doubt about him and about the relationship — wondering if she'd been deceiving herself about the man and had chosen him purely out of loneliness.

DR. LAURA: What about him is giving you these second thoughts?

LILA: The biggest thing is he's a rather cold, remote, emotionally distant person.

DR. LAURA: And you're worried about not being lonely if you live with him? Doesn't sound like a good choice on that level, hon.

LILA: Well . . . we do have some good things in common, but I still feel like I'm doing a lot of work for the intimacy and if I don't, it just doesn't happen. But you know, I just haven't met a lot of men in my age group that I could consider marrying.

DR. LAURA: You still shouldn't be with a man by default! I grant you that everybody has their limitations, but ultimately, being cold, distant, and remote . . . I don't think that should be on the priority list!

LILA: Hmm . . . yeah . . .

DR. LAURA: Does he remind you of either one of your parents?

LILA: My father — in terms of being emotionally distant.

DR. LAURA: Lila, it's not unusual for women to pick a replica of "dear old Dad," because the ultimate in happiness would be if dear old Dad had actually changed to become truly "dear" and nurturing. So to fulfill the possibility of that dream, we try to make the facsimile change or just hope that he will.

LILA: There is something that feels like "home" about him and I'm not sure it's a good thing. But we've never really spent enough time together to call our relationship real life.

DR. LAURA: Please don't move in with him. I would support your relocating only if you get your own modest digs and suggest to him you guys could use some couples therapy.

LILA: Good idea. Thanks, Laura.

I worry about Lila giving up so much in

order to give this relationship a try. Because sacrifice creates an imperative to make it work. And there goes objectivity! Remember, change requires motivation. Lila's boyfriend is in for a big surprise when she lets him know she's not happy with him "as is." Will he be motivated to change? It's a big risk.

THE DAD-AND-MOM FIX

This pattern of women searching for Dad also happens with Mom.

Kathy, forty, described her premarital relationship in a way that stimulated me to nickname it a "rubber-band courtship": Before the wedding, he was constantly shifting in and out of intimacy, and that pattern continued after they'd tied the knot.

When I asked Kathy if there was a lack of loving continuity in her upbringing, she described an abandoning dad and a mom who was usually not around, with some warmies in between. I had guessed correctly that Kathy and her husband there were both wildly tentative about commitment and closeness.

This is how it worked: Kathy's instinctive avoidance of the hurt of abandonment led her to pick a man whose off-and-on behavior threatened to replicate that very abandonment. Ironically, this gave her the opportunity to stay safe. Since he is so iffy, she can justify not getting too close, therefore she can't get decimated emotionally. At the same time, the situation offered an opportunity to make the story come out better.

When she says, "I hate him," she doesn't realize that she's hating her mom and dad. She doesn't realize that the "him" she hates is the worry that she's just not lovable.

BLINDED BY THE PAIN

It is truly surprising how blind you can be to your profound fear of hurt through closeness — so blind that you blame and hate him for the lack of closeness in your life together. That turns out to be a way of not facing and taking responsibility for your inner hurts as well as the means by which you try to protect yourself from those old traumas ever happening again.

The caller named Mary seemed just that blind. She also was thirty-eight and had never been married, but Mary was in an eight-year relationship with a man who, in her words, had "finally agreed to go ahead and get married."

DR. LAURA: *Finally* he's *agreed?*
MARY: He's said he'll get married a couple of times over the years, but he always backs out. And so I am a little apprehensive now. Also, I don't know why, but I don't enjoy our sex life.
DR. LAURA: Well, help me out a little bit . . .

I'm not in your bedroom. What don't you enjoy about it?

MARY: Um, I guess I kind of hold back emotionally because I . . . I don't want my feelings hurt.

DR. LAURA: You don't want your feelings hurt and that's why you're with a guy who's a master of letting you twist in the wind? I don't think you are apprehensive that he won't marry you — I think you're apprehensive that he *will!*

MARY: Hmm, I never thought of it like that.

DR. LAURA: You know what I think, Mary? The problem is not with him — it's with you. This relationship is about how you protect yourself. Withholding your emotions, withholding marriage, is about how you protect yourself. If all this is to change, you've got to be brave and look at how you make distance, safe distance, in your life.

MARY (INDIGNANT): Well, I am not the one who makes distance between us — he is!

DR. LAURA: Darling, you chose him! You've protected yourself right into this situation! That's what you've gained from protecting yourself. And that is what therapy can help you overcome.

MARY: Thank you for being so forthright, Laura. I appreciate it.

So here you have it: You choose a man to rework the most hurtful parts of your personal history or to have it come out better or to protect yourself from getting hurt like that again. And you can't miss hating him on precisely those accounts!

UNCONSCIOUS CHOICES VS. CONSCIOUS NEEDS

Here's another example of a marital situation in which you're unaware how well you have chosen unconsciously but are confounded when that choice doesn't appear to match your conscious needs.

As she came on the air, Ellen, in her early thirties, immediately announced she wanted to discuss parental influence on adult children. What she really meant is that she wanted to talk about her husband. He was from a well-off family — with whom he'd lived until he was twenty-nine — and had a brother who had already made it on his own. Ellen's husband, on the other hand, hadn't accomplished anything to speak of, certainly not as much as Ellen herself, who held a good management position.

When the couple married, Ellen's father-in-law had committed to buying them a house. "So," she told me, "we've been looking and looking and every time we find something, his father finds something wrong with it and won't give us the money." The man belittled and frustrated his son by dangling the down payment before him and then, when he was about to accept, withdrawing it. The son, afraid to confront his father despite Ellen's urgings, took out his frustration on her by "blowing his top."

MY HUSBAND THE CHILD

Ellen was married to a little boy, not an adult, and she knew it. What she didn't know was how to get him to grow up. Unfortunately, as I told her, she chose a little boy, and it's always easier to pick better than it is to change another person. Examined in that light, Ellen's expecting her husband to behave responsibly was basically unreasonable. For the five years she had been with him, she hadn't been a partner — she'd been the parent of an adult child. And I wondered what in her own childhood had led her down this road.

It turned out that Ellen's father, a traveling salesman, pretty much hadn't been there, and her mother — who doted on Ellen's brother — had been verbally abusive and extremely punishing. Now it all began to make sense:

By choosing a totally nonambitious man, Ellen ensured his not being out there in the world — as her father had been. And by selecting someone who withers under confrontation and expresses rage only by "blowing his top," she made sure that the guy was too weak and frightened to abuse her the way her mother had.

What Ellen had done was take two childhood

161

dilemmas, which no longer existed in reality but remained as pain in her heart, and attempted to resolve them through her choice of a mate. Not only hadn't the resolution worked, it had actually created a new adult dilemma. And that — not getting her husband to face up to his father or even steering him toward maturity — was the real problem.

You know the main problem of marrying him to protect yourself from childhood hurts? It's that you end up with a mismatch in the here and now. While your history certainly gives you challenges to contend with in creative ways, you are not now living in your history unless you make choices like Ellen made. It's like a marriage made in a time warp. You are so busy taking care of yesterday that today and tomorrow get overshadowed.

THERE ARE NO SHORTCUTS
TO SELF-ESTEEM

One of the more frequent themes of "women's self-help literature" (and this book too) is self-esteem. Realistically, you can't take shortcuts to it, but that doesn't stop so many of us from trying! Oh, sometimes you get lucky, but most of the time you don't. Let's consider this particular relevant shortcut — marrying from a position of low self-esteem and expecting Sir Galahad to repair it all. And when he doesn't . . . you hate him!

THE DISNEY VERSION

Twenty-nine-year-old Susan claimed that listening to other callers made her feel insignificant, and she hoped I could help her deal with her insecurity and low self-esteem. She'd been expecting her husband to fix them, and that brought only a lot of problems.

When I asked her what form she expected the fix to take, she replied she didn't really know but that she guessed she expected him to wave a magic wand and tell her everything she wanted to hear. But he didn't. Or couldn't. Whatever the case, she was furious.

DR. LAURA: We women saw too many Disney movies when we were kids, because we give men a terrible rap: They are supposed to be and do everything and provide everything, or we get so ticked off.

SUSAN: Yes.

DR. LAURA: Do you realize you came on the program heralding your problem, saying you felt "insignificant"? How have you come to feel that way? Try to answer without mentioning other people.

SUSAN: Well, um, that's hard to do . . .

DR. LAURA: See?

SUSAN: Umm . . . I have done nothing in my life which affirms my worth to myself, I guess.

DR. LAURA: So what are you going to put in

your life that will affirm your worth? Notice I didn't say "who."

SUSAN (AFTER A REFLECTIVE PAUSE): I am a good mom. I have a boy, five and a half months old, and I put a lot of time and effort into reading everything and trying to be the perfect mom —

DR. LAURA: Mistake! You need to be a "good-enough mom" — attentive, loving, and responsive. No one is the perfect mom. As long as you try to be perfect, you will continue to be insignificant in your own eyes.

SUSAN: That's a good point.

DR. LAURA: Give up perfect. I'm not perfect, why should you be? (Both laugh.) Here's your assignment: Think about what you could bring into your life that would convince you — not anyone else — that you have worth. Then call me back. Okay?

SUSAN: Okay!

Now, that's an interesting scenario: not working on your own ego and well-being; instead, projecting that responsibility onto your husband and then hating him because you still don't feel great about yourself.

WHEN HE STOPS TAKING CHARGE AND STARTS TAKING CONTROL

It's not unusual for younger women to try to

facilitate the leap into adulthood through the magic of marrying an older guy.

Heather, twenty-one, has been married three years and has two children by a man who is carrying on a homosexual relationship in their home! She gave up college and her family in the Midwest to go off with this guy, who is ten years older than she and who "took charge of things" and thereby made her feel more secure and settled.

After marriage, the taking charge felt more like controlling. Because of the children, she is focused on getting rid of the other guy — assuming everything will then be "all better." Somehow, I doubt it.

THE MYTH OF MASCULINE POWER

This issue of a controlling man always comes from women afraid of life. At first they see such a man as providing a sense of security reminiscent of when Daddy took care of things — maybe even find him sexy, because he embodies masculine power. Inevitably, when you make this choice and then decide to grow up a bit and start being more powerful in your own life, you become the adolescent child rebelling against the rigid dad — and you hate him.

Briana was walking right into that.

WHY CONTROL FREAKS HAVE APPEAL

Briana's boyfriend had asked her to marry him, but she was having doubts because he was a police officer who worked weird hours and expected her to stay home whenever he was on duty. When I pressed her, she insisted she found his controlling behavior neither romantic nor a sign of respect, love, or caring but saw it as an indication of her fiancé's insecurity.

When Briana asked me whether I felt her boyfriend should be in counseling, I suggested she concentrate on her own insecurity. Honestly shocked, she insisted she wasn't the one with the problem. But, of course, she was. She had chosen a control freak as a boyfriend. In the same way that water seeks its own level, she, an insecure person, had attached to a controlling person who, by the way, was also an insecure person.

Even as we ended our conversation, Briana was insisting that "everything else is so good — it's just that he wants to control me" and assuming (hoping) that marriage would make the whole problem vanish. I could just feel Briana trying to make it all better, using typical protestations of denial such as "Everything else is fine" and "Maybe he'll just stop that after we're married." The first thought is generally, It's really nothing. The second thought, He'll just stop. The third thought, I can fix him. The last thought, What have I gotten myself into?

Too often, hope is just postponed disappointment.

THE BIRD-IN-THE-HAND MIND-SET

There's far too much bird-in-the-hand mentality involved in pairing up! Take Melanie, for instance. She had been married for nine months after having dated her husband-to-be for five years. Before marriage, he'd lived with a group of other unmarried young men who, in Melanie's words, "were always smoking dope and drinking and doing all sorts of things bachelors do." He had, she claimed, a lot of bad influences, and marriage hadn't made them vanish. Melanie took denial to the nth degree!

DR. LAURA: But he hasn't stopped, and he doesn't intend to stop, right?

MELANIE: (Silence.)

DR. LAURA: You ought not to have expected that it would.

MELANIE: I guess deep down I didn't. But I've told him how much this hurts me and how much I think it is hurting him and how, when he does this to excess, it tears my heart out.

DR. LAURA: And he doesn't care much about that.

MELANIE: No. I don't know what to do to get him to stop.

DR. LAURA: Nothing.

MELANIE: I've tried to get him to go —

DR. LAURA: You're not hearing me. I said there's nothing you can do. He's not, never was, motivated to change.

MELANIE: It's just not fair when he does it.

DR. LAURA: Frankly, I don't think it was fair to marry him and expect him to become a new person, either. . . . Melanie, the choice is yours — it has always been. Just like the choice in his behavior was always his.

INSTANT REPLAY: WHY YOU DON'T GIVE UP ON A LOST CAUSE

Melanie's apparent bad choice might be the culmination of her search for proof of her worth or lovability. I know it sounds all backward, but if you've found a parent difficult — emotionally unavailable, self-centered, addicted, or whatever — one scenario for redress is to find someone just as difficult and try to work it out with that person as a final validation of your lovability — like a belated instant replay. That certainly would explain your obvious stupid "choice" and help understand why you cling to it so tenaciously.

And perhaps sometimes you think that even a flaky someone is better than starting all over again — or reaching higher than you imagine you could attain.

MARRYING TO BE WHOLE CAN LEAVE YOU IN PIECES

Up to now I've been pointing out how you marry him and then hate him because he hasn't magically managed to repair your childhood hurts or to make the scariness of life painlessly perfect.

But there are also many women who marry to be a whole person. And when that doesn't happen, the result is hate.

IT FEELS LIKE HATE, BUT IT'S ENVY

Marge saw herself as "melancholic, sensitive, and quiet, putting everyone else first." Then, with obvious disdain, she described her husband as a self-centered type who inevitably put himself first. When I asked her if she could re-describe him — without the insults — as a person who was directed, interested, active, and goes after his dreams, she admitted she could.

The pejorative way in which Marge characterized her husband indicates to me that she covets those qualities she sees in him but doesn't dare strive for them. I suggested she was more than a little jealous and that if she took more risks and made different efforts in her own life, he wouldn't look so bad! And that would mean that she was more satisfied in her own right.

In other words, women tend to try to achieve

balance in their lives by marrying it rather than becoming it. It doesn't work, because the imbalance is in two places. It is within you as you find your fulfillment and personal completion outside yourself in the man of your choice. And it is in the relationship as both you and your man retreat to those polarized corners of being.

HIM AS THE UNACCEPTABLE YOU

Too often, probably because of old parental expectations and the need for approval, women take the unacceptable from within themselves and find someone else in whom it seems to fit. That should mean you're okay because he's not. The point being that you picked him so carefully and then you hate him.

Because the "him" you hate is really the unacceptable you! So the twist here is that you're only okay when he's not.

This "being okay only if he is not okay" is tricky. Heidi, a twenty-nine-year-old nurse, called with a seemingly reasonable complaint about her husband of seven years: obesity. He is 6 feet 1½ inches tall and weighs 300 pounds.

In the first of two conversations, she complained about the possibility that her life might become caretaking a semi-invalid. Being a nurse, she fully understands the health ramifications of gross overweight.

When I asked her more about her history, she

170

mentioned that her folks were alcoholics and that she had repeatedly stayed home to attend to them. Taking a big leap — big risk — I suggested she consider the possibility that if her husband suddenly lost his excess weight, she might actually miss it.

She was unhappy — even appalled — at my words but agreed to think about what I'd said and call back in a week.

She did.

YES, THERE ARE NEW BEGINNINGS!

Heidi confessed that admitting to all those feelings was tremendously painful but revealing, because she'd come to realize that her husband's obesity gave her what she termed the three *C's:* a caretaking role, a controlling power, and a complaining outlet. She now knew that if her husband were thinner, she'd run the risk of losing control and might no longer be able to feel superior to him. Most important, she'd be afraid of not meeting his standards of expectations toward her!

Wow! This was without doubt some of the most intense work I'd ever heard anyone on the air or in my office do totally on her own. What an achievement! And what a wonderful beginning to personal growth — and, I bet, to getting her husband to go on a diet.

NOBODY'S PERFECT —
INCLUDING YOUR MATE

Heidi needed to hate her husband to feel better in herself. Which means you don't always hate the hate. In fact, it can become a treasured possession! Nonetheless, sometimes you simply have to accept the fact that no man is going to be perfect — and that means you don't have to be perfect, either.

DON'T MARRY AN ELEPHANT IF YOU WANT SOMETHING THAT PURRS

Sometimes you hate your men even though they give you what you want — just not in the form you want it in. That kind of pickiness is a definite "cut off your nose to spite your face" attitude.

Janine has a two-year-old and is pooped much of the time. She is really bent out of shape because her husband did not show interest in lying down under the evening stars and chatting with her one evening. I asked her if he had ever been the romantic type and she said, "No, but . . ." It's the "but" that gets you in trouble. If the answer is no, then it is no! He didn't push her away; he suggested cuddling on the couch, watching TV. But it wasn't her romantic vision. She married a nice guy, more mechanical and practical — not an artsy type. And that's fine. It's when you push a man to be other than what he is that he becomes less of who he is. And then you have nothing . . . even though something was available for comfort, which you reject out of your inflexible romantic fantasy.

THROWN FOR A LOOP

Betty, fifty-four, called because she was thrown for a loop. Her live-in boyfriend of one year was doing a big favor for his very ex-wife. Betty was wondering if she had the right to feel angry or jealous or whatever. I asked her if she believed in his loyalty, fidelity, commitment, etc. She said, emphatically, "Yes."

When I asked her what kind of a man he was, she told me, "He plays Big Daddy." I suggested that she enjoyed that quality when he displayed it with her but seemed to want him to change when he was with others. In the course of our talk, Betty realized that the very characteristic she loved about her husband — his big heart — was what she was hating, because she was momentarily insecure.

In the end, they were fine!

WHEN YOU HATE *HIM,*
LOOK INSIDE YOURSELF

When you marry and hate him, look inside yourself first for the source of that hate. If you don't clarify those issues, you may marry and hate, marry and hate, marry and hate — and think that all men are the problem.

THE HAPPINESS OPTION

One final P.S.:

Dear Dr. Laura:

Your comment to someone on your show regarding the character of a person being infinitely more important than their success or accomplishments (something I really shouldn't have to have been told) has cemented in me the greatest love and appreciation for my husband.

I come from a family of outwardly successful individuals, and all our friends make much more money than we do as city employees. For a while I allowed myself to become critical and frustrated until you reminded me that what I have — a true, loving, kind, honest, fun, hardworking, and gorgeous man — mattered most of all. Thanks for that reminder. I had my share of those horrendous roller-coaster high-intensity relationships, until I made a smart intellectual choice to be happy. And it's the best.

Best regards, M.

My dear, you are more than welcome!

7. Stupid Conception

MAKING BABIES FOR THE WORST REASONS

"Obviously, people with life plans have more motivation to control their fertility."
— UC Davis sociology researcher
Carole Joffe
(*Los Angeles Times*, January 6, 1993)

Having used "for the worst reasons" as part of the title for a chapter on conception, I'm left with the arrogant task of detailing what I presume to be the best reasons for having a baby.

Are they, for example: Love? Time of life? Supposed to? Your parents want to be grandparents? So as not to feel left out among pregnant friends? Prove you can? Have someone to love you? Force a marriage? Nothing else to do with your life? Baby as panacea for emotional malaise?

Notice something about all of these most typical motivations? They have nothing to do with the best interests of the child!

APPROPRIATE PARENTHOOD HONORS THE CHILD'S NEEDS FIRST

So here's my notion of the single appropriate rationale for having a baby: You and another adult, committed partner (i.e., spouse) have the interest, intent, ability, and means to make the necessary sacrifices of time, attention, and resources to give that child the nurturing, security, support, love, and education he or she needs!

Procreation has little to do with your needs; it has everything to do with the child's needs.

When you look at making a baby solely from the vantage point of healing yourself, identifying yourself, solidifying yourself in a precarious relationship, or entertaining yourself in an otherwise ho-hum existence, you're terribly disappointed, and the children ultimately pay the price.

THE FIGURES SPEAK FOR THEMSELVES

As I mentioned in an earlier chapter, the Centers for Disease Control report that more than one third to one half of women questioned in a recent survey claimed that their last pregnancy was unwanted or that they became pregnant sooner than desired. The unintended pregnancy rate is substantially higher among women who are young or in the lowest income group or were never married.

I'm still unsure as to what unintended pregnancy really means. That a responsibly used contraceptive method failed? I don't think so. At least, not often. Remember those figures I quoted from the Alan Guttmacher Institute to the effect that of the nation's annual 3.5 million unplanned pregnancies, nearly one half resulted from inconsistent or incorrect use of contraceptives, the rest from using no birth control at all. So much for unintended!

HOW MANY ACCIDENTS ARE ACCIDENTAL?

Of the many, many, many phone calls I have taken from "oops, I'm pregnant" women, most finally admit, after some badgering from me, that they didn't use contraceptives "because . . ." And the "because" too often comes down to an immature perspective of "I thought it would all work out with him."

Sandy, thirty-five, is typical of this mentality. She called me, very angry with her ex-husband! She said he had been talking about their "possibly getting back together." One would hope that would mean counseling or talks about the problems in their marriage and ideas shared about self- and mutual growth, etc. No such luck.

Sandy, despite her initial anger, suddenly began behaving as if "everything were just peachy," as though they were a back-together-and-committed couple! Turns out, though, he already had a girlfriend. Nonetheless, Sandy assumed the reconciliation would all just work out and believed him when he told her he loved her — although he hadn't made a move to break up with his current flame. Sandy was just hoping he'd choose her, and to expedite matters, she got pregnant.

DR. LAURA: How did he react when you told him the news?

SANDY (INCREASINGLY UPSET): He went back to his girlfriend!

DR. LAURA: Sandy, did you have unprotected sex with him?

SANDY: Yes . . .

DR. LAURA: Did the both of you have firm, you know, committed plans to remarry?

SANDY: No . . .

DR. LAURA: How about agreeing to have a baby together? Ever happen? Had he ever independently mentioned wanting a child?

SANDY: No. But he said he loved me!

DR. LAURA: Sandy, that's beside the point. Can't you see that? I don't think your anger is appropriate. You had unprotected sex in a noncommitted relationship with a man who has no discernible interest in having children! So you had a plan, but it backfired.

SANDY: Well . . .

DR. LAURA: Sandy honey, you're in a tough

spot, and you've got some very crucial decisions to make regarding this child. But whatever you do decide, remember this: Never dive into a swimming pool just because a guy tells you there might be water in it sometime. See what I mean?

SANDY: Yes, I think I do. Thank you.

HIS AND HERS RESPONSIBILITIES

Now, here's where the argument can get sticky. It is quite reasonable for you to say, "Hey, wait a minute, Laura! How about the guy and his responsibility!" That's fair. I think every man is responsible for his sperm, where they go and what they do when they get there. The law mandates financial child support; morality mandates actual interaction.

So what!

The 1992 U.S. Census figures show that the problems of single parents today are still, for the great majority, the problems of single mothers. Since it is in women's bodies that the miracle of reproduction takes place and since child care is primarily women's responsibility, I don't think that arguing over men's responsibility actually accomplishes much in the real-world context of pregnancy.

Given that, my advice to you is: If a man refuses to take part in the contraceptive process, refuse sex, dump him!, or make sure you've got Norplant up your sleeve!

179

NO RIGHTS WITHOUT
RESPONSIBILITY

Yeah, I know, it isn't politically correct to hit on the alleged supposed victim, the woman, especially while excusing the guy. There are countless cases where women with children are victimized. However, I've had the opportunity to talk to thousands of women who play director and producer in a plot line that results in children victimized by poverty and impersonal day care.

Tom Bethell, a media fellow at the Hoover Institute, wrote a *Los Angeles Times* essay that contains a thought I wholeheartedly endorse: "Pregnancy involves an antecedent consensual act, and to represent it (or an abortion) as unavoidable is implicitly to dismiss [these women] as lacking free will. Nothing could be more condescending than that."

As women, we can't afford to keep marching for the rights without taking on the responsibilities.

"BUT THINGS HAPPEN . . ."

Then, of course, we have the argument written in a letter by a listener, Rosalie, from El Monte, California: ". . . we are all human, and as such, we make mistakes and have moments of weakness. I agree 100% that birth control is a much better method of controlling one's body

180

— but as they say, 'Things happen!' "

Boy oh boy, if that doesn't consign women to helpless, hopeless idiocy!

Look, forty-six years as a woman on this earth has shown me, firsthand, inequities based on sexism and cruelty based on sexism. But I've also seen it for people of color, Jews, the handicapped, the obese, you name it.

So at this point in my life, after spending the late sixties and part of the seventies angry at men, I firmly believe that women — through their own intelligent and courageous personal, one-at-a-time efforts — can ensure and/or improve the lot of their own lives.

And I am sick, sick, sick of using society or upbringing or anything else to excuse women's stupid behavior. Women must first help themselves, then aid other women, in rising above societal limitations — or there will be no progress.

Many women's groups, even NOW, contribute to the perpetuation of women's victim status by having a political agenda demanding and expecting little personal responsibility, it would seem, from individual women, which, basically, is my focus.

INDIVIDUAL EMPOWERMENT: THE WAY I SEE IT

When I — as a woman and therapist and broadcaster and mother — speak on the air about women's power over their own bodies, I always suggest that the moment of empowerment begins before conception. I have also frequently stated that I believe women, with all that power over bodies uniquely equipped to make babies, are therefore wholly responsible for birth control.

As you can imagine, I've gotten some very heated responses, one from a chapter of NOW — which accused me of, among other dastardly attitudes, absolving men and boys from the shared responsibility for contraception and placing it, unreasonably, on women's and girls' shoulders "in a society that does not sufficiently equip them to protect themselves."

Here we go again with the society-made-me-do-it excuse!

Well, now hear this: I don't think it is unreasonable to expect women to behave with integrity, courage, intelligence, and strength — regardless of the fact that your parents may have bought you Barbie dolls!

It's your body. Take care of it! And if that means not having sex with a guy who won't use a condom, then don't have sex with him! Do not tolerate his cute or callous attempts to get you to relent.

WHAT IF I INSIST ON SAFE SEX AND HE LEAVES ME?

About two years ago I went on the *Geraldo* program to talk about "Safer Sex." The single most frequent question asked me on-camera, off-camera, in the halls, and in the ladies' room was "But, what do I do when he won't use a condom?" I answered jauntily, "Keep those knees together!" To a woman, they countered, "Yeah, but then maybe he'll leave me."

Egad! Is this how far we've come after thirty years of enlightenment? Women may be in Congress, but are they still panicked at the thought of some dude dumping them if they do the right thing for themselves, such as demand he take responsibility by using a condom? Pathetic!

Let me make sure I'm being totally clear. I agree that men should share the onerous responsibility of contraception — of course they should.

But, ladies, wake up. You are the ones who get pregnant. The buck (literally and figuratively) should stop at you!

BRAINWASHED

The arguments against my positions in my listener mail show, I think, that women are defensive because they've been brainwashed and simply accept the "awful plight of women."

Many of you experience and talk of women struggling daily with lousy situations, lousy husbands, etc. Every day I open my microphone reminding women of the power they have in their individual lives to rise above stereotypes and their own weak behaviors. I don't let them off with excuses! I exhort them to use, and to be more responsible with, all the power they have as individuals.

That is precisely why this whole book has been written. I want women to understand and accept that, typically, the mess that is their lives is of their own making. Simple as that. Not society. Themselves.

THIS BOOK IS ABOUT BRAINS AND GUTS

That, in a nutshell, is what this book is dedicated to.

It's dedicated to the type of women I read about who live in a small village in Africa. It seems that this village experiences much marital wife abuse as standard practice. Tragically, this is hardly news, throughout the world or throughout history.

What is news, however, is how the marriage-aged women in the village decided to deal with it: They simply refused to marry! Surely, in this little African village, with no radio and TV, no library filled with feminist manifestos, something special happened. It is called brains and guts!

You know the great quandary at the center of this whole issue? It's why in America, the most liberated country in the world, women are still taking so much abuse from men. It's not because you don't know what's going on — you're anything but dumb. But intelligence is only the beginning. You also have to have the courage of your beliefs, like those African tribeswomen. And I'd like to see women's groups do more to encourage an agenda of personal courage and responsibility.

I hope it won't sound too condescending to suggest that if African tribeswomen can do it, any woman in America, the most liberated country in the existing and real world, can do it!

This was highlighted in a letter I got from a female Japanese immigrant in 1992 (I reproduce it here as I received it):

I am Japanese. I grew up in post–WW II Japan during the MacArthur reign and Hirohito defeat. My culture, then and now, is completely different from this country. From listening your show, I am start understanding about freedom and independent meaning. I was so-called "door mat" my seven years marriage. I didn't have my say, I didn't have my identity, I didn't know how to be in my relationship or total in my life. My family and society are brought up for how to become nice girl, nice lady, nice wife, nice mother, and more you please them you are nice person. No talk back, just support.

I didn't know why, but I need more than that. I choose to come to this country early 1970. Because of my basic instinct, old culture value did hold marriage relationship seven years. Two years of my last marriage time little by little I start make my own identity. Of course, marriage start deteriorate.

Why? I really don't know. It just start like wakening time. My husband likes to make all decision or he has to agree everything, even small detail like pick toilet paper or choose cereal.

First two years of marriage didn't burden me. It was felt even nice to guy to involve making decision in household. I felt strong power in him, that time I liked strong man, so-called "macho man."

But slowly and gradually, I notice my feelings are changing.

I start to discuss with him that difference of my opinion. Of course, he panicked — every time we have different idea or opinion, he has to win. A lot of time I was lock in bathroom two to three hour, he likes to argue and likes to talk, I felt fear first fifteen or twenty minute, so, because he was very angry, but an hour and a half later, he totally convinced to me how he was right, and I was totally agree with him. By the way, he always say, "I can sale ice cream to Eskimo."

But more and more after two to three days, I felt angry. Just like I bought car from use-car salesman with no satisfactory, feeling bitterness left deep inside. My brain agreed once but feeling wasn't, also locking me up in the bathroom felt very powerless too.

Now I got out that relationship, listening

to your radio show, start understanding meaning of freedom and independent. Now I understand why I got out that relationship.

You are like magician. So many invisible psychological heavy tangle, you show like magician do magic. Strengthen out just two second, it is amazing to listening your logic.

Anyway I found out over little two years way from my husband. I met lot woman suffer from spouse abuse. It is mind burst, this United States of America, most a feminist of country in the world, still lot of woman taking a crap from men, psychologically and physically.

I think, we women must wake up, we are human being better know what deserve for our self as equally as man.

I am telling all my friend that if you have a chance, listen on radio at 12 to 2 P.M. 640 AM KFI radio show, because most people just only complain a situation.

I know I made lot of mistake, but at least I know now I am aware of me how I feel. It is great know about this feeling.

Just little bit a neglect, I wish I listening your show and understand your logic before I met my husband. Well! Maybe it was meant be.

By the way, couple days ago, I did go to vote myself. I felt so good, first time in my life I made decision for election and I proud myself.

HOW CAN YOU BE SO CAVALIER ABOUT SUCH A VITAL ISSUE?

I am especially passionate about this chapter because I'm convinced that the contraceptive actions women take — or fail to take — end by affecting an innocent life: the child's.

What follows are the simple facts, as reported by journalist Paul Taylor in *The Washington Post*:

When you have children outside a committed relationship, the kids grow up in a single-parent household — which too often is synonymous with poverty. ". . . Between seventy and ninety per cent of all children born out of wedlock wind up on welfare at some point in their lives, and . . . such children are much more likely to stay on welfare for longer periods than children of divorce.

"In the 1960s," Taylor continues, "there was a global movement away from marriage as the locus of sexual relations. Since then we've seen an increasing detachment of childbearing from wedlock, and we may be entering a third stage in which marriage is no longer the locus of child-rearing. And we're not really sure why all this has happened."

THE ONUS OF SINGLE PARENTING

Well, if our single mom ain't rich, ain't on welfare, then with or without court-mandated child support from the sperm donor, she's probably working and the child is in institutional-ized, impersonalized child care. According to renowned pediatrician and author T. Berry Brazelton, ". . . Children of single parents are haunted by two questions: Why would one parent desert me, and will this one go too? Unless that single parent is there to give the child a sense of how important he or she is, right from the first, they grow up with a pretty flaky self-image."

This is not exactly secret information. So what motivates women to be this non-circum-spect about making babies?

From a letter from a listener: "I hope I can be an example to other women about having babies out of wedlock, for other reasons that are not acceptable. I have two kids, conceived out of me trying to keep a man."

GETTING HIM TO COMMIT THROUGH CONCEPTION IS CHILDISH

Then there was the twenty-five-year-old caller, worried about her unmarried nineteen-year-old sister. The sister has been in an off-again, on-again relationship with this guy, nine-teen. Now she's pregnant. The caller wanted to know the right words to use to convince her sister to get an abortion. She was considering using logic about issues such as finances and education — absolutely the wrong approach!

What we agreed on during the call was to tell

the sister outright that she thought she had found a way to finally solidify her relationship with this young man — a baby — and that it was a very risky enterprise. It's also a perfect example of the immaturity, naïveté, and stupidity all of us women need to talk about openly and honestly in order to educate one another.

BECOME YOUR OWN CONTROLLER!

It is not enough to get in a whiny group complaining about, for example, controlling husbands without taking responsibility for our lack of willingness to take the difficult and uncomfortable role of controller in our own lives. We delegate that role to men willing to play it, then blame them when we don't like exactly how they use that control.

Don't tell me women have no choices because this is a sexist, male-dominated world. That statement would make me — and the millions of women just like me, who made the sacrifices, put out the effort, suffered the discomforts, to get educated and do it on our own, what? — some kind of freak, a member of a privileged elite, or just plain lucky. This is not the case. Not unlike those admirable examples from the ghettos of the world who put in the effort and succeed, we are more appropriate role models.

Because "Do as I say, and not as I do" does not work. You have to live it.

LET'S PUT STUPID BEHIND US

Okay, back to the subject at hand, which is my attempt at highlighting and minimizing typically stupid female behaviors, specifically as they relate to reproduction.

The sexual revolution said we could do *it* anytime we wanted because it no longer meant we were bad girls and because we were entitled to the same pleasures and sexual freedoms as men.

So far, so good. Unless you, or he, are sterilized, if you have intercourse enough times, considering the inherent and real failure rate of any contraceptive (and how lazy and irresponsible you may be with birth control), you will get pregnant. Plain and simple. Then you have to deal with abortion, adoption, single parenthood, or a shotgun wedding.

The equal sharing of contraceptive responsibility and child-care obligations between men and women is not evidenced in the hundreds of calls I have taken from scared, hurt, and crying women when they are "oops" pregnant.

I particularly remember Marie, twenty-two years old, possibly facing a second abortion, who told me tearfully that she didn't want a baby but was scared. The scared feelings actually turned out to be shame feelings, because she remembered that during the first abortion, people had been nice and there wasn't any physical pain . . . but . . . now . . .

191

DR. LAURA: Did you use contraception?

MARIE: Well, my boyfriend and I used condoms, but . . . we . . . we didn't use them that much.

DR. LAURA: Marie, let me ask you something. After you'd been through one abortion, why would you permit intercourse without protection?

MARIE: Okay, we —

DR. LAURA: This is not about we. It's about you!

MARIE: I guess I just got . . . um . . . caught up in the moment! I mean, he was willing to use a condom, but I didn't think I should have to tell him to. It's his —

DR. LAURA: Honey, whatever you do about this baby — and we can discuss the options — I'd suggest getting Norplant, because you are not showing sexual responsibility. You can't let the emotions of the moment overpower you! Look what lack of planning has caused already!

MARIE: Yeah, maybe you're right . . .

MISTAKING FANTASIES FOR ACTUAL POWER

If all that intercourse brought were orgasms, no children, no venereal disease, and no distortions of passion interpreted as love, this chapter would not even be necessary.

As long as there are such serious consequences, we women must act as adults and not as helpless, swept-away fairy princesses. The price is obviously too great for that.

Honestly, I think so many women, including Marie, don't use birth control because they are fantasizing about being in a perfect situation of love and commitment, and they mistake fantasizing for actual power.

USING THE SHOTGUN STRATEGY TO SHOOT YOURSELF IN THE FOOT

Unlike Fantasyland, where "when you wish upon a star, your dreams come true," in real life that's a worrisome gamble.

Michelle, twenty-nine, is an example of that. She's been in an on-again, off-again, sometimes live-in relationship with a fellow eleven years her senior. She laughingly describes him as ". . . a chicken. He's a whole other story. Trust me — you'd die if you knew the whole story of him. It would take much too long!"

It's sad to me that she thinks I'd die if I knew more about this man because he is the man she made a human being with — for the second time. The first pregnancy was aborted some three years ago. This one, she indicated, was a "keeper."

She immediately assured me she loved him with all her heart! She then made it clear that she couldn't get him to commit to marriage — which was clearly why she'd "messed up on the birth-control pills."

Ostensibly, she called because she wanted my advice on how to tell him. She professed to be confused: She didn't want him to *not* marry her. She didn't want him to marry her just because she was pregnant. What she hadn't accepted was that he hadn't wanted to marry her when she *wasn't* pregnant. Clearly, the child was a means to end her boyfriend's bachelorhood. And chances are, even according to her, it wouldn't work.

But that doesn't stop us from trying, does it?

THE ERROR OF "JUST GOING FOR IT"

Doesn't stop us from thinking and hoping that if we "wish" hard enough, all our dreams will come true.

The lengths to which we women may go to enforce the wish boggle the mind and hurt the heart.

Women have a desire, a hope, a yearning, a wish, for a kind of lifestyle. These goals are fine. They help motivate and invigorate.

Yet too many women, running on emotional steam, figure that an emotion of the moment means a necessary action of the next moment. Forget long-term benefits of planning and patience and persistence, let's just go for it.

And this leads me to highlighting other such predicaments women get into when they aren't more circumspect about with whom and under what conditions they decide to make babies.

MAKING A BABY WITH
A MARRIED MAN

One of the more outrageous cases was the woman who had been having a two-year affair with a married guy who frankly said he would never leave his wife. She was upset because the future child's so-called grandparents made it clear they wanted nothing to do with her or her baby.

Now, morally, I have to admit that's somewhat irresponsible, not to say cold-blooded, of them — but what did she expect? There was never any real possibility that her boyfriend would switch his wife for her. Unbelievably, the wife, knowing about the mistress's pregnancy, stayed with her philandering mate!

REMEMBER, IT'S ALWAYS
THE CHILD WHO PAYS

Predicaments? Predicaments!

I'll give you more predicaments. And you'll sadly notice that it is always going to be the child who pays the price.

GETTING LEFT IN THE LURCH — AND FORGIVING HIM

Audrey, twenty-four, had a "boyfriend who got me pregnant, and then split," she complained. Now, what I want to know is, how did he do that without her noticing?

That was about three years ago. During that time she's had a platonic male friend living with her and her baby, being helpful and supportive and acting as a surrogate dad. Now the old boyfriend maybe wants to get back in the picture with her, and maybe not.

She calls to ask, "So, what should I do?"

Doesn't she realize that she is playing games with the child's sense of attachment and security?

A SIXTH SENSE FOR LOSERS

Kathy, forty-one, called with an incredible dilemma.

"My question involves how I should tell my two middle children that they have a different biological father than their older siblings," she said.

She has six children ranging in age from twenty-one to three years, two from her first husband. It's the next two that are the issue.

The third and fourth children were from a seven-year relationship with an alcoholic. "It took me being pregnant twice to realize that I needed to break it off," she continued.

Children five and six are three-year-old twins from her present husband of four years.

The third and fourth children are six and eleven and think that the first husband is their daddy. Their actual biological dad, the sperm donor, was never involved in their lives. Kathy's first husband is listed on the birth certificate and provided emotional and financial support for both of these kids since birth.

"I like this man," I said. "Why did we dump him?"

"Stupid?" she offered, laughing.

One of the rare women to admit to the reality!

She also offered that "life is not always easy."

True enough. So why make it harder?

Why continue to be sexual with guys you know are married, gay, addicts, alcoholics, cruel, noncommittal, not interested in hands-on parenting, violent, etc.?

WHEN YOU WANT HIM TO VANISH — AND HE WON'T

Remember this: When you risk pregnancy with the wrong guy, under the wrong conditions, you'll be dealing with him, or the threat of him, forever.

Ask the women who write me with terrible situations such as having a mean or neurotic or addicted sperm donor chasing after them, wreaking havoc over child visitation and custody. These men don't really want the kids; they are just continuing the sick relationship and escalating it to a higher level of damage and pain.

STOP BELIEVING IN MIRACLE TRANSFORMATIONS!

I've rarely spoken to a woman who didn't admit to "how he was even before." So, please, don't rely on love or hope to produce a miracle cure or transformation. And stop giving in to being scared, weak, or anything else, because that won't stop you from getting pregnant and having to deal with the consequences of that.

Marriage, to my mind, is necessary, but not sufficient motivation or condition to make babies.

ONE WOMAN'S CATCH-22

Brenda, twenty-seven, was "calling because me and my husband have known each other for ten years, we've been married for eight years. My little girl was about nine months when we got married. I got a job at night and came home one night after work to find him with my best friend in the shower. This was eight years ago."

I asked her whether if she gave me the follow-

198

ing eight years of history, would there be mostly things like that to tell?

"Yes," she said firmly. "He's been doing this, and he's been an alcoholic, and he's been treating me bad. I took all his garbage and he said he was going to change."

A month ago, Brenda began repeatedly asking him for a separation because she didn't want him "bothering me and my three kids."

I was thunderstruck! After knowing "what she was living with," she made two more kids with him! Is this the Catch-22 Syndrome of women? You're miserable, so you make kids, now you have kids and you can't get out for the sake of the kids — even though you are miserable with him?

It will come as no great surprise that right after her request for a separation, he professed to be madly in love with her.

That's all it took: All of a sudden, she's confused, unsure about the separation.

As long as he proclaims love, he can torture her to his heart's content. Why do women confuse words with actions? Why do women value words over action?

Because, I think, with these hollow protestations, you get yourselves off the hook from making and expediting brave decisions and behaviors. It always comes back to that!

THE VICIOUS CIRCLE

Many women, as in Brenda's case, continue to make babies as though it were a way of digging in for the winter, to ensure safety and security.

Making babies becomes a way not only of pretending things are okay, but also of trying to force things to be okay, and, perhaps, at least, doing something within this lousy context that *is* okay.

So here we are, though, with children being brought up in a bad situation, which women say they can't get out of because of the children.

Does that really work for you?

THE TIME FOR EXCUSES IS PAST

You must make concrete, rational, intelligent decisions about when and by whom you become pregnant.

No more excuses.

You have the power over your bodies.

I implore you to use it.

8. Stupid Subjugation

LETTING HIM HURT YOUR BABIES

The single most ferocious creature in all nature is a mother whose young are threatened. Ever try poking into a nest with the mother bird close by? Ever experience the rage of a mother bear who believes her cubs are threatened? I don't know how much choice or altruism you can attribute to this behavior. It could be instinct, pure and simple — but just maybe there are love and sacrifice involved, too.

Human beings are the most highly evolved of animals — who have retained only a few instinctive or reflex actions. With our highly evolved cerebral cortex, we can rise above instinct and make choices. That is our glory. And sometimes our shame.

And nowhere is this choice-vs.-instinct issue more evident than in the area of motherhood.

You know, as I write about instinct and choice and the natural inclination to protect our children, I think how mega-totally, how cosmically, I love my own child. If I had to make a choice between anyone or anything and Deryk, it wouldn't even be a choice.

When Deryk was born, I told my husband — the world's most gentle, generous, loving man — that if I thought for a millionth of a second that he might hurt Deryk, I'd reduce him to sub-molecular particles. He said with a gentle smile, "As well you should!"

I remember those several years when my husband and I were struggling to make a baby. I had major surgeries, hormones, temperature charts, etc. At thirty-five I decided I really wanted the experience of pregnancy and mothering — and when that feeling came it was overwhelming.

One night, before I actually became pregnant, my husband and I were watching a PBS program on philosophy and ethics. They were discussing, among other subjects, lifeboat ethics. If fifteen people were on a lifeboat equipped for twelve, what do you do? Dump three people so that the others are assured of survival? Or do your utmost to keep everybody alive and hope for the best?

So, going along with these ideas, I asked my husband, "If, after we have this child, the three of us were in a boat that began to sink, assuming you could only save one person, whom would you save? The child or me?"

My husband, being no dummy, realized he probably could never win this one and declined to answer!

I thought the answer was easy! I said, "I'd save you. You and I have the primary relationship. I guess we could always make another child."

I guess at that point it was difficult for me to imagine the attachment feelings I might have for the child, since he/she was still only a possibility — too abstract for emotional bonding.

Several months later I got pregnant. Late one night I woke my husband with this very earnest question, "Lew, how long can you tread water?"

The question of my attachment and responsibility was no longer abstract. Here was a life of my life, growing in my body — my son. I instinctively knew that this was, for me, the most special of bonds.

And all this from a woman brought up during the feminist years of the sixties who'd thought mothering was some kind of cop-out. What a glorious evolution.

Unfortunately, the whole world doesn't always feel the way I do. All too often, our stupid choices smother our natural mothering instinct and — surprise! surprise! — there's frequently a man involved.

WHEN THE MOTHERING INSTINCT GOES AWRY

Along those lines, I've never been able to forget a case dating from when I first opened my counseling practice. The caller was a woman in her late twenties who had a problem with her boyfriend. He liked her well enough but didn't want her two little kids around — at all. In fact, he was pressuring her to give them away. Her question, believe it or not, was "What should I do?"

That there was even a question was incomprehensible enough, but what followed simply stunned me. Naturally, she didn't want to give up her kids, but she didn't want to give up the guy even more.

I talked with her at great length about love and what it meant in terms of attitudes and behaviors — not just hormones or fearful dependency. I further suggested that adulthood and parenthood didn't feel good all the time but that the long-range gratifications from loyalty, sacrifice, and self-reliance were incredible. I assured her they were the stuff out of which real happiness and self-esteem were forged.

Externally, I was behaving like a calm, rational psychotherapist, but inside, I was seething with rage. How could a mother even consider this choice?

We talked for an hour. At the end of the conversation, she still wasn't sure what her choice would be.

And she never called back.

Was this woman so crippled by desperate need that she couldn't take one step forward? What could have happened to create in her such blind terror of loneliness? I'll never know. But I'll always wonder. . . .

TRAPPED BETWEEN ABUSED AND ALONE

Both on the air and in my private practice, I've always used humor to leaven the mood and make callers more comfortable with difficult ideas and realizations. Even so, one particular call was beyond humor:

Celia seemed at once extremely distressed and emotionally numb as she told me she had married for the second time — she had two toddlers by her first husband — to a man who was physically abusing her and the children. She insisted she didn't know what to do about the situation. When I talked about her leaving, Celia said she just didn't think she could do that — because of the kids.

I asked, "Does that mean you believe it is better that they have a guy who beats them than no guy around at all?"

She hesitated, and said, "Yes."

I was dumbfounded.

I wanted so much to help Celia that I risked sounding nasty by asking her to repeat what she'd said — that it was better to have an abuser around than no man at all. I wasn't trying to be cruel; it's just that I know, as a therapist, that when we hear ourselves say something, it becomes more real, more concrete. And it was crucial that she hear herself loud and clear.

She struggled with the sentence for an interminable amount of time. Then she got going with it: "I think it is better that they have a man around who beats them than no man. . . . no! That's not right!" she screamed into my headphones.

At that point we were both in tears. I gave her a women's-shelter emergency number and some women's support-group numbers, and told her how brave she was. I only hope Celia got the message — and got herself and the kids out of there!

FATAL RATIONALIZATION

At any one time I am talking to only one person. I realize, however, that any one caller represents hundreds or thousands with whom I could be having the same dialogue. So to every woman, to all of us, to each of you, I say:

It is never better — for you *or* your children — to be beaten, terrorized, humiliated, demoralized, or violated than to be alone. Remember, in an earlier chapter, I mentioned how upset I'd gotten at the mother in *Dead Poets Society* who stands by her man at the expense of her son's survival? That's a perfect illustration of such behavior. This rationalization, and that's what it is, comes out of your fears of autonomy and lack of awareness of possible resources.

THERE ARE RESOURCES OUT THERE

Granted, a woman may argue that she's trapped by her lack of education, ability to earn an independent income, or the apparent unavailability of social and community support. Arguably, all these alibis have some grain of truth to them. But there is finally no excuse for jeopardizing your children.

Many women in financial difficulty enter into joint living ventures with other women who also lack extended family support. Others enter programs and shelters. In short, there *are* alternatives to the literally perilous path abused women and their kids are treading. First, you've got to give yourself permission to see that they're there. Second, you must face the fact that there isn't always a neat, pretty, simple way out of the situation — but there *are* ways. If you care about your children, if you care about yourself, you'll muster the courage to do what's right.

But the sacrificing needs to be made by the adults, not by the children — as this next episode clearly illustrates.

ADULTS MUST SACRIFICE, BUT THAT DOESN'T MEAN MAKING THEIR CHILDREN THE OFFERING

A nice couple came in for counseling. Their presenting problem was an inability to budget properly. They would begin businesses, do well for a while, and then the business would go under because of their mismanagement of money.

I suggested they'd be better off seeing a business expert, but they insisted on sessions with me. We kept going in circles, and on the third session I suggested that I talk to each of them alone. I had the feeling I'd been skating on the surface of something important to understand.

She came in alone the next week. I asked her what the secret was. I was not prepared for what she said. They'd been married for twenty years or so. When they first got together, he wanted to start a business so that he would work for himself. She was to help. Then she got pregnant. He was angry about the extra expense a child would bring, and the time it would take out of her being able to help him in his business.

They sold the child. And with that money, he started his first business.

She had wanted to please him, keep him, help him. She said that she figured they could always have another baby. They never did. She said that after all, it was probably her fault for getting pregnant, and she didn't want to mess up his dreams. And she didn't want to lose him. She didn't want to sell the child or give it up, but she didn't know what else to do at the time.

So the choice was made.

The pain and the guilt, mostly unspoken, for

two decades was so great in both of these people that their self-punishing cycles of business failures suddenly became understandable.

WHO SAVES THE CHILDREN?

Sherri began by telling me that she and her sisters had finally admitted to one another that as children they'd all been molested by their stepfather. Although their mother had divorced the man for physically abusing her and had "had a feeling" that something was going on with him and her young daughters, she had never made a move to find out about it. That marriage had produced a son, who now lived with the father.

Through her stepbrother — who hadn't been abused and knew nothing about what had happened to the girls — Sherri learned that her ex-stepfather was planning to marry a younger woman with a small child. Sherri's quandary was whether or not she should tell the prospective wife about the man's proclivities. "I just can't bear to think of having what happened to us happen to his new stepchild," she insisted, "but I'm scared of the repercussion to me!"

I told Sherri that this man rapes babies and beats women and that she had an obligation to prevent his doing so again. Of course, the fiancée will suffer, but she's an adult. She has a choice. Her baby doesn't.

DON'T LET A MAN DEFINE YOUR MOTHERHOOD!

Another caller, Carol, is a repetitively dominated woman. She has two children from her twenty-two-year marriage to a controlling type. Now she's married again, to another man who not only is doing his best to convince her she's incapable of autonomy but won't even allow her twenty-three- and nineteen-year-old children to visit. He is emphatically childless.

"Well, honey, it's ultimatum time," I tell her. "If he chooses to continue this behavior, leave and live somewhere where they can visit. . . . You don't let any man dictate your relationship with your babies. And they're always your babies, no matter how big they are!"

Carol is a mature woman, but she's got a lot of growing up to do. I only hope she does it!

WHEN THE ABUSER IS A HUSBAND, PARENT, OR GRANDPARENT

Women sometimes make extraordinarily sickening sacrifices to appease the "god" — your man, without whom you must feel you can just not live — without the attachment or hoped-for approval. And it can be just as scary, even more so, when the man . . . is your father.

A caller named Nadia sticks in my mind because of her extraordinary detachment while relating a horrendous personal history.

210

She had grown up with a father — to whom she referred as "a dirty old man," although she was irrationally devoted to him — who abused other little girls in the neighborhood. Although he'd never touched her, she knew from her friends what he was doing from the time she was five years old. All the while, her own mother seems to have played — consciously or unconsciously — a permitting role in what went on. Nadia had made a virtual career out of denying her mother's complicity — and almost every powerful emotion she herself had — by becoming "strong in order to survive," cerebral to the max.

Nadia grew up and married, only to find out long after her father's death that he had also molested her daughter — who hadn't told Nadia at the time because she didn't want to hurt Nadia, or affect her sadly unconditional love for her father.

When Nadia confessed she was thinking of writing her story and trying to have it published, I applauded her. For a woman so bound to reason, it seemed an entirely appropriate self-awareness technique.

DR. LAURA: Nadia, that's a wonderful — and needed — thing to do. You need to write to women who put their own children in vulnerable positions with their abusive parents as a way of staying close to that parent. Almost like an ancient sacrifice ritual. You have to do all you can to make sure other women don't do what you did — because of what your mother did before you — letting your need to stay close to Daddy overshadow your maternal instinct to protect your kid.

NADIA: Yes, I think I know that.

DR. LAURA: You need to show them that no matter how intelligent, how "strong" a person believes she is, denial and emotional need can be so great that we put our children in harm's way.

NADIA: Yes.

DR. LAURA: And I think you could do a great service writing it that way. It'll hurt you, make you cry, make you tear your hair out at points, but you could do a great service kicking a lot of women in the butt. And as a consequence of your writing this book, a lot of children might be more protected.

NADIA: Thank you.

THE IRON FIST OF DENIAL

The scary part about talking to Nadia was what she had become in order to be strong and to survive — so removed from her feelings and so unwilling to face the painful truths that she sounded like a therapist discussing a patient. She had actually taken her father's not molesting her as a "sign" of his love, a gift he would never take back.

Surprise, Nadia. The dirty old man appears

to be giving with one hand, but he's actually taking with the other.

FOLLOWING IN DANGEROUS FOOTSTEPS

My caller Linda wasn't able to control the cycle of need, hurt, guilt, and rage. They came out in her nightmares — dreadful dreams in which she repeatedly saw her sixteen-year-old daughter dead or dying. Recently, she'd been dreaming that her now deceased mother saves her and her children from a fire, after which Linda becomes a little girl again, with Mother assuring her that everything will be okay. In the dream, Mother protected her, but in real life, she'd done just the opposite:

Linda had recently begun therapy. Why? Because she and her daughter had both been molested by Linda's stepfather — although she'd insisted she allowed him access to her child only after having been assured he'd been cured!

DR. LAURA: Linda, the dreams are not the point. They are only the means by which you are trying to come to terms with powerful and frightening feelings and awarenesses . . .

LINDA: Yes, I can see that . . .

DR. LAURA: Let me tell you what I think about the dreams. I think they represent your working through your guilt and anger. You do try to whitewash Mom — who on some

213

level was a complicitor to the abuse. You didn't want to lose Mom — so you bet your daughter.

LINDA(SOUNDS OF RESOLUTION): Yes, I did.

DR. LAURA: You are putting yourself through more hell not acknowledging the truth of your mother and the truth of your tragic mistake out of desperate need. What child of any age would find it easy to accept that neither parent gave a damn?

LINDA: I understand. If I kill off my daughter, if she's "dead," then the proof of my mistake is gone.

DR. LAURA: And you also identify with her in that a piece of both of you died with that adult betrayal of trust and protection.

LINDA: It's hard to be angry with Mom, because she's dead.

DR. LAURA: Oh, let's do it anyway. She put her marriage to that bum ahead of her own babies.

LINDA: Yeah, she did. She swept it under the carpet.

DR. LAURA: You are beating yourself up and tearing yourself apart. In your therapy, be courageous enough to deal with this all openly — so you can heal, and so you can help your daughter heal.

LINDA: Oh, thank you so much.

WHY YOU EXCUSE THE INEXCUSABLE

When needs for attachment and acceptance are so strong that rational judgment gives way to fearfully unexamined emotions, the consequences are rarely minor.

Women have called me because they've had abortions solely because "he said to, and I didn't want to lose him." Women have called me because their boyfriends or second or third spouses have gotten "sexually involved with my daughter. I know he did wrong, but what can I do about it all now? I just can't think about being alone again. And what about the finances?" Women have called me because "he's been really mean with the kids. I try to talk to them and tell them that he really doesn't mean it — it's just his way. I just don't know what to do. I really need him."

THE COURAGE TO DO WHAT'S RIGHT

Those needy feelings create an undertow that can pull with frightening power against rationality, disgust, and guilt. But sometimes — due to instinct, character, spirit, call it what you will — we overcome them and make the only decent choice.

Jackie had been feeling desperately lonely, hoping against hope that she would accidentally run into her old boyfriend. She came from a childhood of threats, name-calling, physical abuse, and here was this guy who treated her really well.

So why, I asked, had she broken up with him? Well, there was this one little problem: He had tried to molest her daughter. She'd actually called the police and had him arrested. Now that her daughter had turned eighteen and gone off on her own, Jackie kept fantasizing about readmitting him to her life. You can imagine how I felt about that!

DR. LAURA: Jackie, he is obviously a manipulative creep who makes people feel a certain way so that he can use them. It's typical of pedophiles to schmooze up the mother to get to the kid.

JACKIE: So he picked me because I had a young daughter.

DR. LAURA: That and because you were vulnerable to hearing those nice things. Because without outward approval, you don't feel special or worthwhile. That's the perspective you've got to change, and it's not done through another person — it's done through you.

JACKIE: How?

DR. LAURA: What have you done lately that gives you the most self-pride? Here's one very important thing. I want to tell you that what you did, putting aside your own "sense of security" to protect your child, is truly noble. I've been a therapist for a very long time, and you want to know how many "kids" I've spoken to whose mother made the opposite decision?

JACKIE: No.

DR. LAURA: Don't even ask. But to talk to a woman like you, who was so hurt, so vulnerable, so needy, who still did the right thing — I am very impressed. And I don't think you are appreciating what a thing you did.

JACKIE: I couldn't have lived with myself.

DR. LAURA: And that's real quality of character and courage. So somebody who is going to accept you for what you are — man, you better make sure the next guy knows the quality that he has to live up to in order to be in your life.

JACKIE: That's so nice to hear.

DR. LAURA: My friend, you need to take on challenges you can respect yourself for, in which you come to realize how much you — and others — can count on you. Give it your best. You are already a special lady — you just need to know it better. Call me again.

JACKIE: Oh, thank you.

NEVER BE DETERRED BY FEAR OF BLAME

Don't kid yourselves, mothers, that your children will accept or forgive your weakness or selfishness in not protecting them. Don't kid

217

yourselves, mothers, into thinking that they will see him as more of a bad guy than you — as the cases you've just read about confirm, as well as this next one.

PERMITTING EQUALS CULPABILITY

I was gripped by this news story from the *Los Angeles Times*:

Zelaya's fifteen-year-old daughter, Flora, had been killed while walking the railroad tracks with her sixteen-year-old boyfriend. Did they commit suicide together? No one knows. Zelaya says, "I just know she didn't do it, she was a good girl." Here's something about the good girl's bad life:

Flora was placed in foster care two years before her death, when she was thirteen, after disclosing that her stepfather had been tying her to a chair and forcing her to have sexual intercourse with him since she was five years old. The stepfather was convicted of three counts of felony child sexual abuse and sentenced in August 1991 to fifteen years in state prison, according to the Los Angeles County district attorney's office.

Zelaya had admitted that her husband frequently beat her and her three children, including Flora, with the flat side of a knife, his fists, and the hose of a vacuum cleaner. But she said she had no idea he was sexually abusing her daughter until Flora went to school officials and told them her stepfather made advances toward her seven-year-old stepsister. According to Zelaya, Flora blamed *her* for failing to stop the abuse, and she chose to stay in foster care.

I will never understand why the mother was not brought up on charges of child endangerment for permitting the physical abuse — about which she admits to knowing.

I realize that some of you are now really upset with me for the word *permitting*. The stepfather is the actual perpetrator of the beatings and sexual abuse. If he was the perpetrator, the mother was the one who allowed him to act. She became the permitter.

WOUNDED CINDERELLAS, WICKED STEPFATHERS

We know that people who have been abused as children may tend in some manner to perpetuate that behavior with their own children. Abused boys can grow up to be abusers. Through denial, fear of loneliness, or romantic relationships with men that are really morbid attachments, abused girls may grow up to be permitters of abuse. Hence the many wounded Cinderellas bonded to wicked stepfathers whose stories fill these pages. But self-pity is simply no excuse for allowing children to be harmed!

None of us can eliminate the reality of evil, but we can, as women, avoid inviting it into our homes and beds and when we've identified it, we can make sure not to keep it there. And certainly, we can avoid letting it hurt our babies.

NURTURE, LOVE, AND PROTECT

Moms, don't let anyone hurt your babies and don't sacrifice your babies to make your man happy or to hold on to fantasies of attachment to an evil parent. Nature has entrusted women with the most wondrous miracle: to be able to bring forth new life. Nurture, love, and protect that life.

Keeping or pleasing a man or sacrificing your babies as a Band-Aid therapy for your own childhood pain is not the fast lane to self-esteem. Valuing and honoring your responsibilities is the express route.

DON'T SETTLE FOR ATTACHMENT

A man who would either suggest or demand you do otherwise is not worth the paper he ought to be smudged on. He certainly does *not* love you. He just wants you there to meet his needs. That he meets yours only means you have some clear-eyed soul-searching to do.

When you're stronger, there are a lot of wonderful men out there. I know. I talk to them every day on the air. So stop being so damn desperate!

The price our children pay is much too great.

For years I have been astonished and saddened with the apparent absence of a mothering instinct. One day, I confronted this issue — not as a therapist but as a woman and a mother. I came close to having my head smashed.

My husband, our two-and-a-half-year-old son, Deryk, and I were having a small weekend vacation in beautiful San Diego. We heard of a lovely restaurant, which was a bit nicer than your usual family-style place. We ordered our dinners. I could hardly wait for my salmon, and Deryk was having a ball decimating crackers and breadsticks. (If he's happy, he's relatively quiet.)

It had been a long day, and we were all pooped, so we weren't chatting much. I was lazily looking around the room, people-watching. A family came in and sat down at the round table next to ours. The dad was very tall, a big strong, handsome type with a crew cut. He looked military. His wife was a soft type, brownish-blond hair, print dress. There were two children, a small boy and a girl around eight or nine. Mom and Dad sat at opposite sides of the table, and the boy picked another middle chair while the girl hovered anxiously close to Mom. I heard the girl gently whining to sit next to Mom. Mom didn't say anything. Dad demanded, gruffly, that she sit at the chair to his right, far from Mom. The little girl insisted. He became more stern. Mom sat quietly.

The obviously frightened girl was walking toward me (her dad's seat was back-to-back with mine) to come around him, between us, to take the chair he demanded she go to. As she passed him he reached out and smacked her face sharply with his very large fingers.

My blood pressure spontaneously went up so high my eyeballs nearly became projectiles.

I could not let this go.

I immediately said to him, "How could you do that? How could you hurt her like that? All she wanted to do was sit with her Mom — and now I know why!"

Now it was his turn at boiling blood.

He rose up and started to curse and threaten me with bodily harm.

That he was a complete jerk was readily obvious. It didn't seem to me that there was any point in talking to him without a bodyguard.

I turned to Mom. Frankly, I was more angry with her. And I said, "He's just a jerk, but how can you let anyone, any man, hurt your babies? These children came from your body — how can you let him hurt them?"

She sat there dumbly while he raged on at me. Then she began to mumble something about, "He didn't really hit her that hard."

I came back with "What difference does that make?"

At this point the manager of the restaurant came over, having witnessed the entire event also, and asked them all to leave. It seemed other patrons had observed this family as I did and had commented too.

They left.

The manager conveyed his approval and that of other patrons.

I was so upset I could barely eat my dinner.

When I went back on the air that Monday, I described the situation to the audience and asked for feedback about my actions. Many people were concerned that this would cause the father to escalate later and said I should have kept out of it.

I suppose that is possible. Perhaps it's also possible that the public outcry may have validated the mom's feelings that her husband's behavior wasn't right, and may have given her the strength to do something about it.

At least, I hope so.

The question is: If a mother isn't going to protect her children, should we simply stand by? Where does our responsibility for preventing abuse begin and end? Naturally, there's no cut-and-dried answer, but I have to tell you, I'd intervene again if the occasion arose!

This whole issue of intervention is one I contemplate often. I hope you will too.

9. Stupid Helplessness

"OH, I ALWAYS WHINE AND WHIMPER WHEN I'M ANGRY."

Girl babies know when they're angry. And they have no problem letting anyone around them know that they're angry. So what happens when they grow up to be women and are confronted with a righteous motivation for anger?

Well, mostly self-doubt, whining, whimpering, self-blame, depression, confusion, and lots of other stuff, which has nothing to do with taking on the problem with any objectivity or courage.

FRIGHTENED BY THE FLAMES

Is this because women really don't recognize their own righteous anger? No, I don't think so. When I've probed, nagged, challenged, and nagged some more, I've gotten to the reality of the anger. The main problem is that women are too scared about the ramifications of expressing anger. So they "do" oblivious, confused, hurt, or depressed instead.

Take, for instance, this letter from a twenty-eight-year-old caller who is planning to marry after a year-and-a-half engagement:

> Most things in our relationship seem good except I was wondering about the following: We have good sex. He usually ejaculates too quickly. I usually satisfy myself. He says our sex is great, but he just likes to ejaculate again, so he watches lesbian videos after I go to sleep. He masturbates at least once a day. We make love 2–3 times a week. He has called 1-900-SEX and not told me. Is this behavior good? What could this mean? Help please!

There is so much that is sad about this letter, as well as the sadness it expresses. For example, "Most things in our relationship seem good." Does that convey so much as an atom of enthusiasm? It is such a qualified endorsement. Then, "He usually ejaculates too quickly. I usually satisfy myself." Does it sound as if he's interested in her? No! Just in orgasms — preferably nonpersonal. This is not a guy with a Ph.D. in intimacy.

So she knows she's unhappy and has probably toyed with being angry, but she doesn't do it. Instead, she intellectually wonders what it all means. That indicates that if anyone, especially her fiancé, gives her an apparently reasonable explanation that validates his behavior, she will stuff her feelings of hurt, rage, and dissatisfaction.

Will she then invalidate her own feelings of disgust and perceptions of his selfishness and sorrow over the true lack of reciprocal caring and intimacy? Probably.

WOMEN EXPERIENCE HURT INSTEAD OF ANGER

The central issue here, as I've said, is that women frequently experience hurt when they should be expressing anger. And as long as they are hurt, they don't take any active steps in redressing, improving, or escaping from a bad situation.

HURT MAKES YOU POWERLESS

Hurt is, of course, injury or damage. For our discussion, it is not about a skinned knee or an overworked muscle; it is about emotional pain. The injury is psychic rather than physical. We are hurt by the behaviors of others that are not what we expected or feel entitled to or that demonstrate a lack of caring for us. Hurt obviously indicates a significant degree of emotional involvement and highlights our need, healthy or not, for the other person.

ANGER IS ENERGY

Anger is about extreme displeasure, hostility,

and indignation. Our anger can have many faces: irritation, annoyance, resentment, rage, and fury. No matter the face, the common denominator is energy.

DEPRESSION: THE ABSENCE OF SELF-DEFENSE

When we — or the order in our little world — are threatened, we react with anxiety or anger. These are internal mechanisms that help us mobilize to protect, defend, and reestablish our sense of safety and control. In the absence of self-defense, there is depression.

In depression we simply come to accept a situation in a passive-submissive way. It is far healthier to rise up against the injustice and demand redress or change. It is far healthier to walk out in the face of prolonged lack of redress or change.

LEARNING TO ACT ON RIGHTEOUS ANGER

Although healthier, it is not necessarily typical female behavior to get in touch with your strongest feelings.

I was struck by the caller Judy's sadness as soon as she began speaking. In a voice tinged with sorrow, she described a situation that would create turmoil in anyone. About three years previously, when she was in her

227

mid-forties, she had confronted her father with the fact that he had abused her as a child, and he had admitted it. Subsequently, though, he recanted, claiming she was making up the entire experience. And her mother sided with good old Dad.

At that point, Judy had requested that her husband sever all connections with his father-in-law, and it seemed he had — until Judy discovered they had recently spent time together. Now she was feeling "very depressed and down" about things. Depressed and down — but not angry? When I suggested that too often women substitute depression for anger, she agreed she did feel some anger, too.

JUDY (NOW WEEPING OPENLY): I've told my husband before that I think it's betrayal, him seeing my dad.

DR. LAURA: But, Judy, you feel it and you think it and you've told him, and he does it anyway. And the reason you went into depression is so you wouldn't have to face that. Right?

JUDY: That's true. That's true.

DR. LAURA: Well, enough of this depression. You've suffered enough. Do not acquiesce to other people's selfishness!

JUDY: Okay. How do I . . .

DR. LAURA: Well, you could start by telling your husband that he's loyal to one or the other, and he'd better choose right now or he is out. . . . I have a feeling that the disloyalty in this one episode is not something out of the clouds.

JUDY: No, it's not.

DR. LAURA: Okay, Judy. This is a form of abuse, in my opinion.

JUDY: Right.

DR. LAURA: So sit up straight! No more depression!

JUDY: (laughs)

DR. LAURA: Judy, your anger is righteous. It is real, valid, justified. Act out on it . . . and I don't mean you pop him on the head.

JUDY: (laughs)

DR. LAURA: You tell him to choose — or he's history. And I'm sorry about your mom and dad, but not all eggs and sperm come from people with the honor and integrity and courage to really be parents.

JUDY: It's just like — you still want their love.

DR. LAURA: Forget it! They don't have lovingness to give — except toward themselves, if you can call it that.

JUDY: Right. Okay.

DR. LAURA: So, no more depression. Say, "Laura, I'm angry."

JUDY: Laura — I'm angry!

DR. LAURA: Hooray!

THE PASSIVE-SUBMISSIVE PERSONALITY

The ultimate sadness for me is to hear how people refuse to stop trying to get love and approval from bloodsucking, slime-producing, im(or a-)moral, insensitive, unloving, uncaring, self-centered, disgusting sperm and egg donors (aka lousy parents). And the all-too-typical next step, after you're weaned and out of the nest, is to continue that hopeless crusade through a very similar spouse, which is a new, warped definition of *normal*.

That's when I get mail like the following from a fifty-year-old woman whose husband has been blatantly fooling around with a next-door neighbor for eight years!: "I went to three psychologists and two self-help groups trying to fix why I was so paranoid about this arrangement my husband had . . ."

That is an all-too-typical scenario for women: Blame yourself. It's safer, frankly, than putting the blame where it belongs and risking intimacy and vulnerability with healthy people. It's easier, it is believed, than fighting through the fear, pain, and loss to become healthier inside yourself.

DESPERATE ATTACHMENT

In addition to the safety of the passive-submission technique of not risking the pain of change or loss, there is another important explanation to the "it must be me" syndrome of handling someone else's inappropriate behaviors: Sometimes too much of a woman's identity, like that of a child's, comes from a desperate attachment to a male. That means *his* actions are inexorably connected to *her* self-worth.

Sue's boyfriend also calls the X-rated 900 sex lines, and it's making her feel just terrible — about herself.

DR. LAURA: Now, instead of going, "Oh, is there something wrong with me?," I want you to stand back and ask yourself, "My gosh, do I want a guy who does this? Yuck. Do I want this guy to father my babies?" Now, why do you think you went immediately into the "What's wrong with me?" mode?

SUE: Because . . . well . . . I always think it's me that's wrong.

DR. LAURA: You are really not answering the question. Your reaction is always "What's wrong with me?" I'll tell you, Sue, what's wrong with you. You are so desperate to be wanted by a guy that you almost don't even care what kind of a guy he is as long as he wants you. You are not choosing. You are sitting there hoping to be chosen.

SUE: Yes.

DR. LAURA: That's the problem. You are too needy of the attachment.

SUE: Okay.

DR. LAURA: An independent person would have stood back and said, "What a jerk."

SUE: Right.

DR. LAURA: Confronting him about the phone sex is an entire waste of your time. I wouldn't bother doing it. You simply have to say, "I am a mature woman and I have respect for myself." (You might have to fib a little here, Sue . . .)

SUE: (laughs)

DR. LAURA: . . . That's good practice. "Do I want a man who engages in these kinds of behaviors — do I want it? Regardless of whether he wants me — do I want this kind of man?" And then, Sue, you answer that question. That is what an independent, mature woman would do right now. You have the opportunity to be one of those.

SUE: Okay, got it!

GOING ON OFFENSE

Have you noticed how women jump right into the defensive position? If you got into the offensive position, your man would probably know he had someone of quality to contend with. That's assuming he is up for that kind of challenge. Granted, I can't promise you a 100 percent success rate, but I can assure you that the more you practice self-assertiveness, the more natural it becomes.

My caller Sylvia claimed "to have a pattern of getting my hopes set on men who hurt and disappoint me," and she gave me the following example: About a week earlier, she had phoned a man she had first met through her church but whom she hadn't seen in a while. They had a habit of going to lunch after services, so when he said, "I'll see you in church," she figured that meant lunch. But when Sunday arrived, he was there with another woman.

DR. LAURA: Sylvia, you just assumed something. And hopes, dreams, and fantasies have no power. If you want something, you must be willing to express it.

SYLVIA: Yes, I realize that.

DR. LAURA: I'm not sure you do. Because when you say "disappointments," there is a difference between somebody's being concretely disloyal and his not having the vaguest idea what is in your head.

SYLVIA: It does make me see that I've done this before. How do I break this pattern?

DR. LAURA: You say, "I'd really like to be with you in church and go to lunch like we used to." And then he would have to say that he'd like that or that he can't due to a prior engagement or that he's got a new honey or whatever. But you have to say what you want, think, need, feel. You have to be willing to do that.

SYLVIA: I know that this is the nineties and

women have permission to do this now. And I have taken the initiative in this relationship more than he has. So I think I have gotten the message that he is just not that interested.

DR. LAURA: Well, you know, not everybody has great taste!

SYLVIA: (laughs) You're nice!

DR. LAURA: Let's hold out for one who does and let's be real clear as to who Sylvia is and what she would like. You have to be assertive in your own life, my honey.

SYLVIA: Okay, I'm trying to learn that more and more all the time! Thank you.

And that's just about a date. Sometimes it is about a whole marriage.

FAMILY FEUD

Lee called me in tears over a family matter. It seems she and her husband had started their own business a few years earlier, and at her husband's insistence, his brother and sister-in-law were hired on the assumption that eventually there might be a second store, which they could manage. And it hadn't worked out — in spades. Not only did the couple have to be let go because of their incompetence, it subsequently turned out that they had embezzled money from the business — although Lee and her husband had decided not to prosecute, for the sake of the family. Now Lee was going to be forced to attend a family Easter celebration with "those people who have hurt us."

I wondered if *hurt* was really the word. It wasn't. She was furious. Furious because she'd been against hiring the in-laws initially but her husband had insisted. Furious that they were able to screw her over, and she'd been too wimpy or careful or timid to handle it up front.

"I'm not sure which it is," I told her, "hurt that they screwed you or anger that you feel powerless to do anything about it because you're afraid to cross your husband." I advised Lee to do something active in terms of confronting them, if only to demand a family mediation session. Because staying in a one-down position wears on you — whether it's with people who betray your trust or husbands who make the decisions regardless of your own feelings and intuitions.

SUPPRESSED ANGER KILLS

According to an article in the *Medical Tribune News Service*, "Suppressed anger may increase the risk of death from heart disease or cancer. Married women who suppress their anger are at the greatest risk of premature death. For wives and women there is a direct relationship between suppressed anger and mortality, more so than for men."

And women do suppress their anger — out of

worry about direct confrontations or negative exchanges, about not seeming nice or feminine. You worry about rejection and criticism. You worry so much that instead of showing righteous anger you cry, act injured, sulk, get depressed, exact small, nasty, subtle revenges, and generally suffer. And, according to the above study, get sick and die.

THE ORIGINS OF TIMIDITY

Alicia, forty-seven, is a successful businesswoman, but she has one trait that makes her feel bad about herself: She doesn't "have the courage to tell people what to do." She was even afraid to tell her cleaning lady to park in an alternative space so that Alicia could park in her own garage space. Why? "I would end up feeling very guilty for hurting her feelings," she said.

I told Alicia that she was not "five years old any longer. Your parents are not going to keep your allowance and put you in your room without supper. You see, you are talking from the vantage point of a little girl whose welfare is totally dependent on the goodwill of her parents. Now you are a grown woman, and other people have to count on your goodwill. It now goes two ways. And you haven't updated yourself to the adult stage of this. In your mind you are still the five-year-old girl who is afraid of getting Mommy and Daddy ticked off!"

LOSS OF PARENTAL ATTACHMENT: A CRIPPLING FEAR

And that is just where it is. Women get afraid of hurting people, because people will get mad — and if people get mad, people will reject or punish. And all will be lost! You will be lost!

While I feel and believe that the special affinity women have for relationships and attachments is lovely, too much of a good thing can be bad. When women are afraid of losing any attachment, no matter how insignificant (I know a good cleaning person is hard to find) or dangerous or destructive or unfulfilling — it's gone too far.

And that goes for relationships with parents, too.

As a matter of fact, that's where it all begins. And when it doesn't end well there, it can go on forever.

Theresa, my twenty-seven-year-old caller, was fear personified. She was so frightened, she wasn't even making sense — at first. Once she settled down, I learned she still felt guilty about leaving home to go to college against her parents' wishes and never returning on a permanent basis. Still, she was close to her family and deeply aggrieved (and guilt-ridden) by the recent death of her dad. Theresa had a good job, with potential, and was living with somebody. The somebody turned out to be the problem. She'd started dating him — probably, she suggested, as "a crutch" — around the time of her father's death. Now he was pushing for marriage, but his insecurity and extreme dependence on her put Theresa off.

DR. LAURA: You don't sound like you want to marry him. In fact, you sound like you'd rather he just go away.

THERESA: (laughs) But he is so dependent on me.

DR. LAURA: Like your parents — your family is, too!

THERESA: Yeah, I suppose.

DR. LAURA: Yeah, so you've had all these people pulling on you for their needs — their needs — and you feel guilty wanting and putting yours first. Your punishment for leaving home — your father dying — is getting yourself stuck with this guy who is just like your family!

THERESA: Yeah, I suppose.

DR. LAURA: Why don't you finally be definitive?

THERESA: Yeah, I guess.

DR. LAURA: If you would permit yourself the luxury of being honest right now.

THERESA: All right! I want this guy out! I don't want to hurt him.

DR. LAURA: Theresa, there is no life without pain — and the experience and the survival of pain are often the price of growth.

THERESA: Right.

DR. LAURA: And the measure of you as a

valuable, lovable person is not that you don't cause pain. There is a difference between intentional viciousness and the pain others quite reasonably feel when they don't necessarily get their own way — or have to face their own weaknesses. That is just a normal part of life — a necessary hurt.

THERESA: So what do I tell him?

DR. LAURA: That you regret not sharing his desire for commitment and marriage — and the relationship is over. I think you are basically afraid to have your own desires put into action lest you be seen as bitchy or selfish.

THERESA: That's what I've always been called when I do it.

DR. LAURA: Not by me!

THERESA: Okay.

DR. LAURA: I hereby give you, Theresa, twenty-seven years old, who has struggled these many years, permission to assert your individuality, to make the decisions that you wish. You will be more of a giving person if you are in a place where you really want to give. The kind of giving you are doing now is acquiescence, not giving.

THERESA: You're right, thank you.

INCLUDING YOURSELF IN THE EQUATION

There is a big difference between cooperation out of respect and submission out of fear of rejection. Women need to believe — or, until that point, just take as a given — that they, like every other human being (including parents, siblings, spouses, friends), may assume the privilege and power to be a unique individual in their own right. This doesn't mean eternally running rough-shod over others; but it *does* mean including yourself in the equation — and not as a leftover, a byproduct!

So that when people take outrageous liberties, when they betray trusts, when they display ongoing total disregard for your welfare, when they use and abuse you without remorse, when they refuse to accept responsibility for any of the pain and devastation you suffer — please don't just sit there and eat, drink, take drugs, sleep, or work yourself to death to avoid the reality that they don't care.

DOWN WITH "THE BENEFIT OF THE DOUBT"!

It is so painful to witness this denial and pale attempt at giving other people the worn-out benefit of the doubt. Is it really that you are not getting through due to bad syntax? Is it that your voice is modulated too low? Is it that his hearing is damaged and he can't hear female higher-pitched sounds? No! No! No! It is that he doesn't care and he knows he can get away with it!

NEVER AGAIN!

That's where anger becomes important! It sets limits, it puts the other on notice that there are consequences, it says, "Never again."

You must give up the illusion that service to the dominating needs of others brings love. The fantasy of winning approval or love through long-suffering toleration of others' single-minded self-centeredness doesn't bring in the love of others. And it promotes the hate of self.

COURAGE: THE INSTANT CURE

We misplace the anger when we are afraid of seeming inadequate by showing our hurt or vulnerabilities, when we are afraid of anger, disapproval, or punishment. The instant cure is to use your courage to speak up directly and find, to your long-term, infinite pleasure, that you can and will live through it!

WHEN ANGER DOESN'T BELONG

Having said all that, I admit anger isn't always righteous. It can be inappropriate, invalid, wasted, or misdirected — even sought after.

SETTING YOURSELF UP TO BE MAD

Yes! Much too often, women — due to the "I am attached, therefore I exist" utterly nutty romantic concept — actually set themselves up for hurt and anger in their relationships with men.

For instance, showing interest in all his things as a way to catch him. But then, what have you got? A partner? A friend with mutual interests and respect? No way. Then you spend the next twenty years being mad at him because you feel like your interests don't count.

As I've been saying in chapter after chapter, women tend to make a relationship their life, their identity, while men make it a part of their lives. So women are constantly angry at men for not being caring and intimate.

Recently, a caller described herself as "melancholy, nurturing, caring, and sacrificing," and described her man succinctly as "self-centered." Not an uncommon complaint. I asked her if he could also be described as "energetic, involved, active, outgoing," and she answered in the affirmative.

Women, fearful of risk, often pick such men to attach to in order to complete themselves from the outside. Through him, the woman vicariously experiences the qualities she dares not risk. The problem comes when she later vilifies the man for the same qualities that initially attracted her.

There are no two ways around it: Women must have more dimension in their lives than "loooove!"

INVALID ANGER

Remember Janine, who had asked her husband to lie outside with her on the grass and watch the stars? He suggested instead that they watch TV together. She called me because she was "terribly hurt by his rejection." I asked if he had ever been the laid-back or romantic type. She said, "No, but . . ." (I always stop women at the *but,* because it is just an attempt to erase the full realization of the answer: No.) I told her that she married a wonderful elephant and was now irked that he wasn't a kitty cat, purring in her lap. No fair!

That's not an unusual scenario for what I call invalid hurt. Here's another:

GIFTS WITH STRINGS ATTACHED

Vicky, twenty-five, has been married for three years and feels something has changed about her husband's unconditional love for her since she became his wife. "Before," she tells me, "he used to appreciate me. I don't feel he does anymore. . . . Every time I try to do something nice for him there is always, instead of thank you, some kind of negative." She claims she's afraid to do things for him for fear of doing them wrong and making him angry. Now comes the killer example!

In the process of making chicken soup, Vicky asked her husband if he wanted the skin left on. He said he didn't know. But she persevered and nagged and nagged — until he finally started to scream, "I don't care." "I would have screamed at you, too. Nobody likes to be nagged," I tell her, before giving my interpretation of the situation.

Granted, this guy could be a complete S.O.B., in which case Vicky should lose him, but here's what's more likely behind his actions. There is a notion about doing things for someone as a gift and doing things for someone to entice or manipulate him into seeing you in a certain way or behaving in return in a certain way to fill you up. It is a seduction, not a gift. It is a manipulation, not a gift.

THE TELLTALE IMBALANCE

If, over a period of time, a man feels as if you are not really giving but that you are trying to manipulate him into changing or doing something you want, he is going to get more and more resentful. Vicky's husband may be gaining resentment over her behavior. Either that is a valid part of what is going on — or he is a creep.

Either way, the doing-for and buying are certainly indirect ways of asking for something. It is out of our vulnerabilities and weaknesses that we treat others in ways we call giving, and then watch, perplexed, as the recipients' resentment and annoyance mount. That is the telltale imbalance that leads me to say that Vicky's husband is not registering what she is doing as giving but as her attempt to get something in this indirect way, which always leaves him feeling inadequate to meet her demands.

STACKING THE DECK

Jicka, twenty-four, is suffering from the same syndrome. She called to ask how one recovers from being cheated on. She said that her boyfriend had a date, probably sex. I asked many questions, and here's what I learned: They have no spoken agreement for a commitment or even sexual monogamy. In fact, she has made it clear to him on innumerable occasions that she has no intention of marrying him (defensive fib).

When I suggested that cheating in these circumstances was not possible, she was shocked by my answer. She had really hoped to get complete loyalty and fidelity, giving nothing back but guarded distance! Then he proved her worst fears about men: They can't be trusted! Talk about a stacked deck of cards! Talk about testing under totally unfair parameters.

HURT REACTIONS

These are some examples of unfair, inappropriate hurt reactions — which are not hurts in-the-now but reverberations of attitudes and hurts from the past superimposed on unsuspecting subjects.

Inappropriate Anger

Anger can be inappropriate or unfair. Lisa, twenty-five, has been in a seventy-five-mile long-term relationship with her boyfriend for two years. He doesn't want them to move in together and he is not ready for marriage. He enjoys their relationship and has been up-front about his feelings and intent. And Lisa is angry.

I suggested that if he were being evil, cruel, manipulative, devious, or whatever, her anger would be appropriate. As it was, she didn't have the right to anger, since he'd been honest all along. Disappointment would be more appropriate.

In point of fact, Lisa's not really angry with him, she's feeling unfulfilled as a person and imagines that marriage will fix that for her. Therefore, his resistance stands in the way of her fulfillment, safety, identity. So she is livid!

I suggested that her anger toward him ought to be redirected toward her own personal growth. Such a lot of repressed anger, when used to fuel personal growth, could give her the energy to do some really spectacular achieving.

Belinda, forty, has been married for twenty-two years and has three kids, six, fifteen, and twenty-one. Since 1988, her husband has been romantically involved with another woman. When Belinda found out about the affair, he didn't apologize for the incident but "only said he was sorry that I got hurt." Even now, every three months or so, the woman's phone number shows up on Belinda's bill. "I feel like he's doing this on purpose," she insists, "to punish me for whatever."

DR. LAURA: Now, that's interesting — for punishment. I think he's doing it because he simply wants to, and he can do it and get away with it.

BELINDA: And I don't want him to be able to do that anymore.

DR. LAURA: What are your alternatives?

BELINDA: I have children, and, um . . . stay or get out.

DR. LAURA: That's right. You're not going to change him; he's not willing.

BELINDA: No, he isn't.

DR. LAURA: So if you want or feel you need to stay, say to yourself, "Self, I'm making a choice to stay for the security of the kids." And then get off the case.

BELINDA: Dismiss it?

DR. LAURA: Well, if you are determined to stay for the security of the family, you might as well accept it. Understand that you are making a choice and a sacrifice — we all have to make 'em in life. When you make them, you have to truly accept them. And you still haven't accepted the choice you've made, because it is the one-down position of no power. I understand that. You are trying to change him instead — forget that. But do use condoms if you continue to have sex with him.

BELINDA: Thank you, Dr. Laura.

Mind you, I am certainly not condoning this man's behavior — I'm trying to save Belinda from a heart attack. And sometimes, when women *really* settle down with the reality of their predicament, they choose *not* to settle for the predicament. Instead, they become more motivated to do something about it. But not when the anger is misplaced.

Misplaced Anger

Sally is five months pregnant and also has a toddler in the house. She called because she is being "so bitchy" to her husband. She wants to know why. First she says, "Everything is just fine." It took me a while to get to: "Well, I'm tired all the time, we're not having fun like we used to, there seems to be so little time for affection and sex."

She is certainly feeling the weight of parental responsibilities and is not dealing directly with the changing needs of her life and how they are colliding with her personal needs. Women often don't like to admit they can't "handle it all." So they act bitchy.

I asked Sally to talk to her husband directly about the fears, the losses, the worries, all of it — and I was certain she would find he shares the very same feelings.

WHY HISTORY REPEATS ITSELF

To recap: Our early childhood attachments, love, and nurturing experiences will teach that we are lovable and that emotional attachments are generally safe and rewarding — or the opposite. If it is the opposite, then we come to expect such things as hurt, loss, betrayal. When we are in that mode, it is amazing how history seems to repeat itself with future adult relationships. And we are constantly hurt. The anger that might have seemed so appropriate to the situation is squelched by the incredible self-doubts, which lead us to feel we have no right to anger — we just aren't worth it.

AMEN

Yet the only way to become worth it in our own lives is to believe in some kind of universal inalienable right to respect, honor, commitment, caring, and love — and then to earn it in our own minds by our courageous efforts in our own behalf in just about every aspect of our lives: work, relationships, and love. Brave choices. Brave actions. Self-esteem earned. Amen.

I want to leave you with the story of Judy, twenty-eight, who is humongously off the mark when it comes to what to be angry about.

She just found out her fiancé has a five-year-old child whom he doesn't see or support financially. Judy is angry that "the relationship can't be that close if he didn't trust me to tell me." I suggested that if she were planning to make babies with him, she ought to be more concerned that he did nothing to fulfill his parental obligations and responsibilities in an honorable way.

She seemed not to react much to that. She was more concerned about her security within the relationship than with noticing the quality of her future husband.

Oh well.

10. Stupid Forgiving

"I KNOW HE'S ADULTEROUS, ADDICTED, CONTROLLING, INSENSITIVE, AND VIOLENT . . . BUT OTHER THAN THAT . . ."

Have you ever noticed how motionless a praying mantis remains, no matter what is going on around it? The only creature capable of equaling that limitless patience and tolerance is the human female — who will invent millions of excuses to avoid getting out of the way of an oncoming bad relationship or permanently escaping from one in which she's already ensconced.

These excuses encompass protestations of practicality and unselfish love, obligation and commitment. Since they are all lofty ideals, they make a good defense.

If you have the courage to dig a bit deeper, you'll find fear, self-doubt, avoidance of discomfort, and ingrained habituated patterns of relating that have been in place since your childhood family dynamics.

THE PRACTICALITY PLOY

Let's start by exploring practicality. Anita called to talk about the balancing act she was attempting to pull off between her pot-smoking husband and the ex-husband with whom she has sex now and then. We discussed the alternatives of personal as well as marital therapy, status quo, or leaving. She didn't like any of those. She had a million reasons why she couldn't/wouldn't change any part of or the whole situation.

A few weeks later an articulate, heartbreaking — and clarifying — letter arrived from her. In it, she explained that she had married her "not-so-good" second husband, the pot smoker, so that her kids could have a full-time mom as well as a dad who provided for them. She stayed with the doper because "a loaded dad is better than no dad at all." If, at this point, you think you're experiencing a sense of déjà vu, relax; the "any dad will do" excuse is one of the major themes you've read about in this book.

She agreed I was right when I told her she needed to find a sense of purpose, but claimed she just wanted to be a good mommy to her girls. Then she continued:

I've wanted them to have what I didn't have — parental attention, a family home life, some new clothes once in a while, a decent car and house, help with homework, socializing — just the normal things a kid deserves. I am perfectly capable of going out into the world and getting a decent job, but I like being a homemaker.

I am not expecting my ex-husband to rescue me. I think, rather, we are both rescuing each other from a loveless life — even if it is only for a few hours a month. It is a sad thing to live without loving. Sometimes you (ME!) seem to disregard the realities of life and its complications.

For those of you who have done things in the proper order (education first, then career, and children later), the world may not seem so frightening. For those of us who must face the future with many hearts depending on us and being ill-equipped and knowing it, the choices are not so simple.

Anita.

I realize that such a letter could make a houseplant weep. Luckily, I'm a totally heartless and cruel therapist who only wants people to get better and be happy, so I wasn't about to fall for it.

UNWILLING TO CHANGE

Basically, Anita isn't being honest with herself. Granted, she wants things to be different in her situation so that she can be more content. But — now comes the "hook" — she is totally unwilling to change anything. Oh, of course, there are excuses and rationalizations, but what it all adds up to is "How do I change this without touching it?" But why?

As I have said at many a counselor training session and civilian speaking engagement, most of our problems don't come from being stupid or insane but from our attempts to solve other problems. It's just that the side effects of such solutions are immobility, frustration, and unhappiness. By now we've built a house of cards. If we remove the bent card, which obviously has to go, the whole structure might collapse. So we stay and feel stuck.

TRYING TO SOLVE THAT OTHER PROBLEM

The situation Anita actually wanted to resolve had less to do with her children's welfare than with her own unhappy, apparently isolated childhood. So she made babies with a fellow who invoked her parents' emotional distance, then sacrificed for the kids in exactly the way she wished her mom and dad had done for her.

That may seem to benefit the kids, but it's sure not good for her.

MAKING PEACE WITH YOUR TRADE-OFFS

For everything there is a price. Your sanity and inner peace come from recognizing, accepting, and paying that price. Therefore, my advice to Anita is this:

You must make peace with your choices and trade-offs. A change in attitude can mark a change in happiness — and this attitudinal change is your only option if you're unwilling to change anything else about the situation.

There are times when such trade-offs — staying in a not-so-good situation for reasons — will be your choice. The point is that you need to make the choice consciously and maturely. If you don't, you leave yourself open to disappointment, frustration, anger, and hurt.

In which case, you are not a victim, you are a volunteer who is not behaving maturely.

CHANGE OR SHUT UP!

Generally, women resent and resist the idea of acknowledging up front what you are in reality accepting and putting up with anyway! Do you think constant protestations of victimization and unhappiness absolve you of responsibility for your choices? Do you think if you complain or whine loud or long enough, things will change all by themselves?

Forget about it!

RECYCLING IS ABOUT GARBAGE

Liz, thirty-nine, has been in what she considers a relationship with a fellow for six years. They have a four-year-old daughter — or, rather, she does, because he split right after that fertilization. Liz is both resentful and confused because the man repeatedly comes in and goes out of her life for sex, money, a roof over his head, some attention, whatever, and then slides right out again when someone or something else more interesting comes along.

Talk about a commitment to recycling!

Liz expressed so much annoyance and confusion at his most recent vanishing episode that I was shocked. Why, I asked her, was she so "surprised that a gorilla was eating another banana?"

How blinded by fantasy can you be! Get real, girl!

WHEN NOT CHOOSING IS EASIER

Of course, it is the facing of reality that causes the most fear and pain. And sometimes, not choosing is easier than changing. To avoid the pain, you've got to do something: anger, drugs, food, affairs, depression, physical illness, toying with suicide, perpetual recovery groups — something!

However, the real challenge is confronting the realities within you.

ENSURING YOU DON'T GO BACK

So let's say you do that. You face the music and leave. Now what do you do to ease the pain of the emptiness? You fill it with giving and growth, learning and creating.

Without doing these things, as you will see later in this chapter, you'll probably yearn to go back into that bad relationship situation, repeat it with another guy, sit with sadness and regret and imagine you've probably made a mistake.

SHE LEFT, AND SHE'S STILL MISERABLE

For instance, one woman called me on the air yesterday to say she left a rotten relationship because she thought, "I'd be happier once I left. And I'm not." I told her that she left "to have the opportunity to build happiness."

Leaving is not enough. Happiness is not a given, nor is it automatic. It is hard-earned.

DO I HAVE THE RIGHT TO LEAVE?

Now, if you suspect you are in a bad relationship situation and are playing with the idea of getting out, you may be struggling with the question "Do I have the right not to want to stay?" Like Kay.

Kay is a forty-year-old mental-health professional who is married for the second time — to an alcoholic. Whenever she insists he stop drinking, if only for the sake of his two sons from a previous marriage, he insists she's blackmailing him. At this point, she is serious about giving him an ultimatum and leaving if he refuses to get help, but she feels guilty.

Kay's husband is undermining her resolve by tweaking her typically female sensitivity about hurting others and demanding too much. Mix that in with the anticipated discomfort of change and loss, and you have the formula for questioning your right to leave.

Therein does lie an important key: preexisting self-doubts. In Kay's situation, you have notions of repetitive marital failure, the impact of turning forty, and professional doubts about having used the wrong "technique" on her husband.

IS SOMETHING WRONG WITH ME?

Usually, however, the doubt is more basic: Is something wrong with me? That's what Susan wondered.

Susan got right to the point by saying, "My husband has some sexual desires which I don't like and just won't participate in." These activities — in which he was pressuring her to participate — included group sex and watching him have sex with other women and with men. She knew she was at a crossroads in the relationship and would probably end up leaving. So why had she called? She wanted my reassurance that not giving in to his demands didn't mean she was sexually dysfunctional.

What I told Susan is that the sexual issue was actually not relevant. If she was being urged to do something she felt was wrong for her, she had every right to decline. "Susan," I said, "you are entitled to live the kind of life you want. It simply doesn't matter what he says is normal sex. If you're asking me if there's justification for leaving, well, I'd have to say there's always a case to be made for leaving an uncomfortable and unpleasant situation."

THE SELF-DOUBT COP-OUT

"Slipping someone a mickey" of self-doubt is the way controlling people like Susan's husband exercise much of their power: "You'll never find anyone to love you more than I do"; "If you don't want to have group sex, no man is going to want you"; "You're much too (fill in the blank)"; "You'll drive everyone crazy"; etc.

Sadly, the technique is generally a sure-fire winner when used on women, whose sense of self and value is measured too much from outside acceptance. But there is one plus: If you can make a connection between your need to be controlled and childhood trauma in a therapeutic context, it could be the key to understanding and conquering misplaced shame and guilt.

STAYING PUT DESPITE THE PAIN

Without therapy, those personal early-life losses, and the desire not to repeat them, provoke you to question whether or not you have the right to leave.

When you wonder if you have that right, it's not so absolute a judgment as one might think. It really depends on your baseline, or what seems more normal or expected.

For example, a private patient of mine spoke of being physically abused by her husband. She was well educated and gainfully employed, and I wondered why a woman with no children who was capable of financial autonomy would tolerate this situation for as long as a second. She looked at me through her tears and explained, "Well, he beats me less than my father did. So for me, it is an improvement."

An improvement! How sad a perspective.

Unfortunately, this woman is not the exception. There are countless others who are also not even thinking about leaving — but they should.

IT MUST BE MY FAULT

There is Aurora, who for over three years had been going out with a congenital — not to say pathological — liar. Why did she call? To ask if I thought *he* needed counseling! I observed that he wasn't the one who had called, so he probably didn't feel strongly motivated to change. She, on the other hand, was. But Aurora wasn't really hearing me — until, in answer to her repeated attempts to get me to talk about his problem, I responded sarcastically, "It must be your fault!" Then we started to get somewhere.

DR. LAURA: Aurora, this is an issue of your self-worth.

AURORA(CRYING): That's what I've been told by my family.

DR. LAURA: But you don't listen! You want to make this an issue of what is the matter with your boyfriend? Okay, he is sick. And you are overwhelmed by your fear of being alone, of loneliness. As long as you can worry, forgive, and caretake him, you never have to be alone, you never have to grow, you never have to face your worst inner fears.

AURORA: That's true.

DR. LAURA: He's an excuse and a way you hide from yourself, honey. But you are the one who will pay the price.

AURORA: You are right.

DR. LAURA: And you must believe there is a time coming in your life when you will know how valuable you really are. Right now you don't. I'm going to give you a therapist referral. Interested?

AURORA: Yes, yes I am.

DR. LAURA: Great. But, Aurora, nothing will change until you acknowledge that in your benevolent martyrdom to this man — who will always disappoint you — you are only running away from what can become your greater self. Make that phone call!

AURORA: I will! — thank you, Laura.

TRYING TO AVOID THE INEVITABLE

Carol, twenty-eight, has another motive for not even thinking about leaving — when she should be fleeing for her life! She had been married for ten months to a man she described as "this person." She even had a baby by him. Only after the marriage did she find out that he had, as she described it, "a felony record." When I pressed her, she admitted his offenses included strong-arm robbery, petty theft, and "something where he has to register as a sex offender."

DR. LAURA: What? Carol, you just made a baby with this guy. If he rapes and/or molests, then this child and you or others may be in some kind of danger.

CAROL: Right. Well, he says . . .

DR. LAURA: Whoa. You know, when women say, "He says," I get scared. Because that's usually a woman who doesn't want to think for herself.

CAROL: Yeah.

DR. LAURA: That's a woman who, if he says the right thing, makes believe everything is all better.

CAROL: Yeah, well, I also found out that he lies all the time.

DR. LAURA: Carol, why are you still with this creep?

CAROL: I guess I feel like a failure in my marriage.

DR. LAURA: A failure? Your husband is a blot on society, and you feel like a failure. You made a mistake, Carol. That's not the same thing as failing. Failing is staying with him and risking the welfare of you and your child! Use some objectivity here. Now, Carol, do you want to compound the mistake? Or do you want to get smart and get out?

CAROL: I'd like to get smart and get out.

DR. LAURA: Then do it.

CAROL: I . . . I just don't want to hurt him any more than he has already been hurt.

DR. LAURA: Don't give me "You don't want to hurt his feelings" — he's earned whatever consequences he gets. That is so typically female! No matter what horror he perpetrates, you don't want to hurt his feelings by telling him he's hurting you.

CAROL: I'd have to go to my family in northern California. I'd be taking his son away from him.

DR. LAURA: Carol, this guy is a sex offender, not a pillar of the community. You could well be doing your child a favor, at least for now. And right now what you and the child need is the roof, the food, the support. And you need counseling, with some distance to give you objectivity. Go home! Okay?

CAROL: Okay, Laura.

I must admit, after this call I put my head down on my notebook during the commercial break. This much voluntary blindness was difficult to bear. It isn't anger I feel at calls such as this. It is intense emotional pain. And it is out of that pain that this book was conceived.

STUPID IS AS STUPID DOES

Women, in my opinion, aren't in these predicaments out of stupidity. Remember the title of this book refers to stupid behaviors, not stupid women. Women are more likely to get into these predicaments because of their orientation toward life, which has less to do with inner courage, independence, and individual creativity than it should.

HOW CAN I EVER TRUST HIM AGAIN? I'LL FIND A WAY!

Tammy, twenty-eight, is married to a man who's a repeat offender in the infidelity game. Granted, he straightens up and flies right every once in a while — when Tammy threatens to leave. But she stays put, and he reverts to type. She called because the guy had a job that wasn't within commuting distance, "so he's

264

gone most of the week," she told me mournfully. Clearly, her question for me was "How can I trust him?" And there was no response to that. But what she really wanted me to know was she felt she "had nothing, was nothing."

DR. LAURA: You have yourself. That's not nothing. You forgot that, though, didn't you?

TAMMY: Yeah, I gave that up a long time ago.

DR. LAURA: Well, get it back! You know what you're going to do? You are going to get busy on your life. When you make him your life and you fear losing him — and sit there and say you have nothing — that scares me. He is supposed to be a partner — he is not supposed to be you! You are supposed to be you.

TAMMY: Every time I try to start something, he would do something to undermine me.

DR. LAURA: You have to remember that you are not a slave or indentured servant; you are not owned by him. He is not your father; you are not a minor. You are a grown woman and you make your own decisions. You have to get that back in your mind. You need something of your own to feel good and strong about.

TAMMY: Yeah, that's true, but when I first got out on my own before, I had some bad experiences so I more or less hid behind him.

DR. LAURA: Well, don't take that typical female escape route again, because you only end up losing yourself — totally.

TAMMY: Well, he knows if he fools around again I'm gone.

DR. LAURA: He doesn't have any reason to believe you will.

TAMMY: Yeah, that's true.

DR. LAURA: Now, let's talk about your dreams and your interests. I bet we can get a reality-based game plan going. Okay? . . .

HIDING BEHIND HIM

Hiding behind him. Sad. And bad. Aside from the obvious reasons why, think of the kind of man you get when you pick a hiding place. It's certainly not going to be someone desiring an equal, open, mutually respecting relationship — is it? No, of course not. You'll end up with someone who gets off on being one-up.

And the behavior of a "one-up" type is not going to feel that good to you on the receiving end. You do not have any bargaining power at all, because you are so inappropriately dependent. At those times, you have to accept the trade-off.

ISN'T IT HIS MOVE?

Ann, fifty-five, has been married almost three decades. She's always suspected his affairs, but unfortunately, now she has concrete evidence. The pretense of all these years is not so easy for her to maintain — it is just getting too blatant. So she tries to salvage by asking, "Well, doesn't it mean he loves me if he hasn't asked for a divorce?"

No, of course not. This is not a man who loves. This is a man who possesses and keeps power over women in various forms. Ann is struggling to keep the fantasy of a relationship going, somehow. She asks, "Well, isn't it his move to tell me he wants a divorce?"

No, of course not. He's got all he wants. He is not the one dissatisfied. This is Ann's life — she's the one who is supposed to make decisions for it.

She toys momentarily with the notion of a divorce, then thinks about the physical, tangible, practical elements of her life — the money, the house, the "family," and the general social structure — and thinks out loud how she doesn't want to lose all of that. Then she says, "No, I think love is what I want and need."

"But, Ann," I answer gently, "those two things, security and love, will not occupy the same space at the same time in this marriage. Pick one."

And she picks the one she's always picked — security.

So I tell her, "Dump your concrete evidence and forget it."

THINKING YOU'RE A VICTIM DOESN'T MAKE YOU ONE!

I just don't consider Ann a victim, except of

her own unexplored, undeveloped, and untapped inner self. And that is a tough concept to get across to women who proclaim to be hungry and open for love and intimacy while camping out in a barren desert.

So many women call with this complaint: "If it weren't for him . . .", as though they had no choices! If you want Chinese food, it seems foolhardy to me to go to an Italian restaurant and scream for years at the chef about why there are no dim sum on your plate! Right? Right!

THE PROBLEM IS NOT THE MAN

Women, look within. The problem is not the guy — it is the way you have chosen to solve the problem of your fears about intimacy — by not really risking any. And this self-protective, predictably disappointing predicament is whitewashed with "But I love him."

DESPERATE DEPENDENCY

Please. You are not talking about love — mutual regard, admiration, respect, thoughtfulness, openness, acceptance, honesty, etc. — you are talking about desperate dependency, a sad attachment of familiarity.

Familiarity can be a deadly trap. The convenience, the routine, the time invested, the daily structure, provide an intense pull. Combine that with a fear of the unknown both in the world and in yourself and you have a recipe for quicksand. You're just not going anywhere.

What motivates moving on? For some, the pain of where they are just gets too great. For others, it is the glimmer of hope and the attractiveness of new possibilities, provided by role models and books like this.

HAVING A MAN WON'T HEAL YOU

Having a man won't heal your hurts, resolve all your self-doubts, and protect you from life's challenges. The kind of man you pick while you're in that mode is not one you would recommend to your best friend. Admit it. Face it. Do something about it.

Or you may end up hurting more than yourself: Like Aurora, Carol, Tammy, and Ann, Sandra is too afraid to think about leaving — but she should!

UNDER HIS THUMB

Sandra began by saying she was thinking about putting her son into therapy because of the havoc wreaked by her marital relationship. What she really wanted was to get her overbearing husband into treatment, but the man, who is in total denial, claims he doesn't need it, that everything will be peachy keen if "I just listen and obey him."

And I tell her: "Whoa! You need to tell him

that that's all well and good, but right now you are dealing with certain things in your interactions, which have nothing to do with doing things correctly, that are diminishing your feelings of love and attachment. Ask him if that is of any concern to him.

"Tell him you need him to come work on these things with you. The ultimate reality is that if he refuses, because he doesn't take you seriously or is too scared and therefore stubborn, that this goes to the extreme — leaving."

Sandra must stay focused on her personal perspective — as a responsible adult, not as a little girl under Daddy's thumb. Her marriage is in deep, probably irreparable, trouble. Sending her eleven-year-old to therapy will be relatively useless unless his home situation considerably improves. Whatever old patterns are being acted out through her being dominated, Sandra — with professional help — must learn to take charge and make changes, for the good of her son and herself.

SOMETIMES YOU DON'T WANT TO SEE

A call to action. Finally! So why didn't all those women see clearly that they were in the wrong place? It's not a question of not seeing — it's not *wanting* to see. Let's face it, change is difficult, painful, scary. The devil you know is always better than the one you don't.

THE DREAD OF LETTING GO

This brings us to the dread of letting go and moving on. There are many styles of this literally paralyzing anxiety. Here's a sampling of them:

The People-Fixer

Fixing a man is the way some women try to affirm a self. Holding on to a man is the way some of you basically define a self.

Barbara knows what to do — but she is frightened. It is sad how women can let being scared become the predominant force in their lives. She has been going with a very dependent guy, who's pressing for marriage — despite the fact that he has never made love to her and doesn't plan to. Far from wanting to marry him, Barbara really wants to end the relationship — but she is a "people-fixer." She seeks out the needy in order to avoid fixing herself. It's time she got to work on that and stopped even considering sacrificing her own happiness for someone with a serious hang-up whom she doesn't even want around.

Saved by the Tooth Fairy

Suzy has been separated for two years because "he won't let me go." I laughed and told her that this was not the reason she was still separated but her excuse. Some women stay connected just in case they can be saved by the Tooth Fairy, or whoever. Suzy's husband is an alcoholic with a bad temper. He doesn't get any help, just comes back and forth with promises and disappointments. But Suzy keeps hoping that next time will be gold.

After a while she stated the real fear: "What if I can't find another man?"

I guess it would be the end of the world, gravity would cease, and the entropy of the universe would go for broke.

Fairy Tales Never Come True!

Linda's husband has always had affairs, even during her pregnancy. She spoke to me just before she was to give birth and had gotten the resolve, finally, to file for divorce. The divorce, with the substantial financial settlement, will be final in two weeks. Now he is being, in her words, "perfect." She wants to know if she should stay out or not. I mean, it would be nice if fairy tales did come true. Let's face it, ladies, seducers are good at their job — with their wives and all their other women. They know how to tell you what you want, what you need to hear.

He's a Louse, But I'm Lonely

Bobbie, fifty-two, has been harassed for many years by her drunken ex-boyfriend. She sounds as if she is angry with his recurrent attempts to connect with her. But then she admits that she becomes open to him because she gets lonely, and welcomes even this sick attention. To her, I say: "You're never too old to get a life. Go do it, and you'll find yourself shedding your neediness."

The Dancing Yo-yo Master

Heather, twenty-four, has been in this relationship for ten months, during which time he yo-yos her with closeness and carries on with at least one other woman. He gets called on it or caught red-handed and cries. She is beguiled by the tears. I told her to keep focused on the behavior between the tears — it counts more. It's the tears that give Heather the momentary longed-for belief that he wants her.

She is too hungry for that moment.

But He's Not All Bad!

Lisa is also feeling very conflicted. She's been separated for one year and has two children, five and six. That makes the picture muddier. She admits he is a good dad, a good worker, and has been faithful. As our dialogue continued, it became clear that he didn't make a good partner.

His insecurities led him to be so terribly controlling that he lost all sight of compassion. His neediness was destructive. It was hard for her to stay out because of his "good qualities" and entreaties that he had changed.

Lisa's brother has a terminal illness, and several members of the family want to take him on a trip to Europe before he dies (which will be soon). Her husband, emphasizing all the changes he has made, had demanded she choose — the trip or the marriage.

I thought that made the decision to stay out easier.

So did Lisa.

ONCE YOU'VE MADE THE MOVE . . .

So let's move on to what happens once you've made the decision to leave.

You've had the good sense and guts to stay out. And, then, within days or after many years, you have those terrible second thoughts: Maybe you've made a mistake. What might make you think that?

MAYBE I'VE MADE A MISTAKE!

Pat had broken off a relationship five years before, and now she was having second thoughts. Under my prodding, she revealed that the guy hadn't wanted to get married, was unemployed and on drugs. So why in the world did she want such a no-goodnik back? Well, it seemed he'd gotten his act together and was doing well. She, on the other hand, had done nothing with her life and had a job that she found unfulfilling.

DR. LAURA: You look back at this guy, see that he pulled his act together, and you go, "Oh gee, maybe I should have stayed." You were intelligent to leave when you did, but you haven't done anything with your life. So you are looking for some guy whose nest you can go into.

PAT: Right.

DR. LAURA: And then what? You think that alone will make you happy?

PAT: No.

DR. LAURA: Yes you do! You think that will save you and make you a fulfilled human being.

PAT: So I should just make myself happy, right?

DR. LAURA: Go make yourself feel like you have purpose on this earth. Go feel like your existence makes the world different. Go do something that gives your life meaning. Your choice in men will improve. We only go after, and we only accept, what we think we deserve. Go back to school — go become yourself. Dream, reach.

PAT (WEAKLY): Okay.

DR. LAURA: You sound so unmotivated. And you tell me *he* didn't want to make a commitment? You aren't willing to make one to yourself! You are asking for somebody else to do for you what you won't do for yourself!

PAT: I realize that.

DR. LAURA: I know it is scary and tedious, but go do something. . . . The rewards are great.

PAT: I will. Thank you.

Pat made the right decision leaving the wrong

man. That step is necessary but not sufficient for a fuller and happier life. It's like cleaning out the cobwebs — now you've got to paint! The leaving gives you the room you need to grow — now you've got to get into the process of growing, learning, taking on challenges, and taking new risks as you work toward your dream.

And, frankly, a guy who "pulled himself together" wouldn't be too interested in a woman who didn't do the same!

I KNOW I SHOULD HATE HIM, BUT . . .

Janet, forty-five, also made the smart move of leaving and, like Pat, is having second thoughts. This time the reason is that she doesn't know any other way of relating to a man other than being his "mommy."

Janet's is a twelve-year live-in situation with an alcoholic drug addict who "borrows" money (sometimes with permission) but never repays, and who doesn't keep any responsible work.

"I should just hate him, but I just sit here and cry," moans Janet. "I know I did the right thing by throwing him out. . . . I just keep wanting to call him."

Janet's challenge, now that she did the right thing by leaving, is to be brave enough to grow from where she is in her own mind and heart: believing that being someone's mommy is the only way to ensure some security in the attachment with a guy.

If she, at forty-five, is too scared to deal with that, she'll continue to have these second thoughts.

For Pat and Janet and too many of you, second thoughts become a welcome relief from change.

WHEN STAYING CAN BE THE RIGHT THING

Finally, I want to mention two reasonable, major motivations for not leaving, even though it would seem, at first glance, the right thing to do.

For the Sake of the Kids

Lisa, thirty-one, admits that marrying was a "business arrangement." He got a mother for his two kids; she got the financial security she desired. She has been having some sexual flings for "emotional and sexual" satisfaction — he knows all about it.

Then this call took a twist! "I don't want to leave the children. We are very close. Their mother abandoned them completely and I don't want to make them go through that again by my leaving. I love them," she related.

I was most impressed. Here is the moral trade-off point. The benefit of being a parent, of nurturing and experiencing the wonderful feelings of a warm relationship with children, was her number one priority. She was willing to accept the reality of that trade-off for what she

277

felt were the unbeatable gains.

I told her I admired her.

That's one important reason to stay when you ordinarily should leave. Kathy has another.

When the Problem Is Partly Your Fault

Kathy has been married for almost eight years. She relates going from one dependent relationship to another, like a rebellious child. And here she is again. She says her husband is critical and controlling. She realizes that her dependency made her pick him — but now, she says, she's been changing and growing and no longer needs nor wants his "type."

She has been totally withdrawn from him, communicating and sharing nothing of her thoughts or feelings. He's read her journal to find out what's going on with her, and Kathy is furious.

I told her that she went into a game with him and now changed the rules. I would suspect he's quite hurt and feels rejected. If someone married me for the qualities I had and then decided later that these qualities were despicable and withdrew from me, I'd feel hurt and sick and nervous too!

"So you need to have some compassion for his position," I said. "Instead of looking at him as your enemy, a controlling S.O.B., you need to look at the reality that you didn't want to make choices in your life — you wanted to make someone else responsible, and that was what you opted for. You owe him frank discus-

278

sions about what is going on, to see if he could also evolve. He's not the enemy. He's not the one who has been keeping you back your whole life. You were!"

So Lisa is staying for the children — for their personal benefit and for the satisfaction it gives her. Kathy should at least stay long enough to have one experience in which she does not behave like a rebellious child as a means of showing or experiencing independence.

ALWAYS FOLLOW YOUR SMARTS, NOT YOUR FEARS

I have often said on my program, "Water and self-esteem seek their own level." That means that when you are with a man who does bad things (violent, negative, controlling, addicted, illegal actions, etc.), your mixture of compassion ("He's really got a good heart underneath") and reticence ("Oh, I'm just too scared to leave; maybe it'll get better . . .") demonstrates that you don't think much of yourself or your possibilities in life.

Well, women, the only way out of that is to follow your smarts and not be led by your fears. Do what you would recommend to anyone else — leave, grow, change, take on challenges. Do something obviously constructive. That's the way you impress yourself into better self-esteem. Stop resting on the wilted laurels of being an adult child of (fill in the blank). That just keeps you weak.

Follow a game plan with courage, grit, guts. That's the way any of us finds satisfaction, ultimately.

Do the right thing . . . and don't tell me you don't know what that is — I know better. Don't let fear, laziness, or cowardice be your Pied Piper.

I know you can do it. Hey, I'm counting on you! So get ready, get set, and go take on your life!

P.S. Here's an extraordinary item from Ray Richmond's television column in the *Los Angeles Daily News*, which highlights the lack of conviction in too many women:

"If you watch tonight's edition of the syndicated *Night Talk with Jane Whitney* talk show, you'll see a North Hollywood couple named Marla Young and Kenneth Makley participating in a theme show about 'Men Who Won't Commit to Marriage.' "

Young called to note that she has issued Makley an ultimatum: Commit to get engaged by Christmas Day or else.

Or else what?

"Or else . . . I'll get upset," said Young. "But I won't leave him no matter what," she added.

"Now," concludes Richmond, "there's a woman who stands by her convictions!"

Epilogue

THE BIRTH OF THE SMARTS

So what do I hope you've gotten out of this book? Simple. I hope it's jump-started your courage; that it's made you aware that you must stop acting stupid, that you must get smart and come up with unique solutions to your personal situations. Your behaviors have to change, and that means taking leaps and risks that are, I admit, scary. But look at the alternative. After all, you've been living with it.

Recently, I've listened to far too many women callers absolutely marinating in their history, writhing in misery because nothing has changed even though they've had the Therapeutic Insight or attended Adult Child of Whatever meetings for a year. The real key to growth, as these women know but fear to face, comes from within, not without. It is doing something new and different for yourself, something that will challenge you to rise above where you're at now in your soul.

In May 1993, I gave a talk to a group of working moms and received only a 50 percent approval rate. In fact, the room seethed with hostility as I endorsed the absolute necessity of babies being with mothers and/or fathers who attend to them and provide the love and positive feedback they need to grow and mature in good emotional and physical health. A good number of the audience members who attacked me, it turned out, were women who had made babies with bum husbands who then left them, one-night stands, men with no intention of committing, married types, guys with serious hang-ups, etc. The so-called victims of these turkeys claimed I just didn't understand that society, social services, etc., weren't set up to allow them to be proper mothers, to "do the right thing" by their kids. According to my detractors, all I was doing was laying guilt on them.

"Well," I countered, "I'm not about to take responsibility for the stupid, irresponsible behavior that landed you in your no-win situation in the first place — or for the rotten luck that undermined your best-laid plans. I am, however, willing to discuss the need for creativity and determination in finding a way out of your pain."

Just a week ago, at another public appearance, I was approached by a young woman who had attended my Working Moms lecture. She had, she told me, been among the angry ones, but she had subsequently realized that her resentment was really about trying to affix blame on someone beside herself. Since then, she'd taken my advice to heart, gotten smart, and created a gourmet-lunch-delivery business, which, since it operates out of her home, allows her to be with her child. She had started out resenting me bitterly. Now she was thanking me sincerely. Truly, that touched my heart.

I assume that many of you who have read this book are also angry at me.

Yes, I know that females who are sexually abused or who have been raised by single/never-married mothers often become sexually active too early and end up being single moms themselves — in a desperate attempt to repair hurts and make a special connection. My hope is that, if this profile applies to you and you've made it through this book, you are now motivated to shift gears and move in a positive new direction toward self-determination and fulfillment.

The current feminist agenda mostly accuses men or society in general, thereby ignoring the pivotal role played by women themselves in their life predicaments. What I'm asking of you is to acknowledge to yourself that all persons on this earth confront challenges — willingly or unwillingly — and that some of these challenges are uglier than others. Let's face it: There is no destiny outside of what you give up or take on.

With this book, I passionately want to help you face your inner and outer demons and lay claim to your own lives. I want you, through your courage and compassion, to begin to build a better, richer existence. Once you take the first step, you will experience a "ripple effect" in which more strength brings better choices, which leads to greater satisfaction for you and for those whose lives you touch.

This book, to me, is the first pebble thrown into the brook to make those ripples begin.

Twenty-two first steps for women to take when they decide to get smart

TOLL-FREE HELPLINES

Attorney Referral Network
800-624-8846
24 hours

National Council on Alcohol & Drugs
800-475-HOPE
Information on local treatment centers; literature

Child Abuse
800-422-4453
24 hours
Information; referrals to local agencies; crisis counseling

National Council on Child Abuse, and Family Violence
800-223-6004
Information and referrals on child abuse, family violence

Credit
800-388-CCCS
Information on local credit counseling services

Domestic Violence National Hotline
800-333-SAFE
24 hours
Information and referrals for women abused
verbally, mentally, or physically

Eating Disorders
800-382-2832
24 hours
Information and referrals

Mental Health (National Clearinghouse Family
Support/Children's Mental Health)
800-628-1696
24 hours
Information and referrals

Pregnancy
800-238-4269
24 hours
Information and counseling to pregnant women;
referrals to free pregnancy testing; foster and
adoption centers

Sexually Transmitted Disease
800-227-8922
Education; information on sexually transmitted
diseases

Youth Nineline
800-999-9999
24 hours
Referrals for youth or parents about drugs, homelessness, runaways

HOUSING RESOURCES

ACORN
202-547-9292
nonprofit network of low- and moderate-income housing

MISCELLANEOUS SELF-HELP ORGANIZATIONS

Rational Recovery
916-621-4374
Helps achieve recovery from substance abuse and other compulsive behaviors through self-reliance and self-help groups (nonreligious)

Women for Sobriety
800-333-1606
Helps women achieve sobriety

Debtors Anonymous
212-642-8220
Recovery from compulsive indebtedness

Gamblers Anonymous
212-386-8789
Recovery from compulsive gambling

Sexual Compulsive Anonymous
213-859-5585
Recovery from sexual compulsiveness

Compassionate Friends
708-990-0010
Support to families bereaving death of a child

Share
513-721-5683
Recovering from violent death of friend or
family member

Abortion Survivors Anonymous
619-445-1247
Recover from impact of abortion on self
and relationships

Survivors of Suicide
414-442-4638
Helps families and friends of suicide victims

Widowed Persons Service
202-434-2260
Peer support for widows and widowers

(Associated with AARP)